This is a delightful book, a scintillatingly original nature story that will engage readers on multiple levels. Belinda Probert's erudition, verve and wit enables her to reveal and transcend the challenges that confront even the most sympathetic and open-minded of northern hemisphere migrants when trying to gain a full imaginative grasp of Australia's testing landscapes. Raised to love the pastoral rural scenes and picturesque garden settings of England, she engages in a deep, lifelong, intellectual and emotional mission to understand and appreciate Australia's unique flora and fauna, as well as our associated human cultures. In doing so, she takes us on an exhilarating journey that also leaves us a great deal wiser.

Iain McCalman

Imaginative Possession:
Learning to Live in
the Antipodes

Belinda Probert

Belinda Probert grew up in the Weald of Kent, wanting to be a sheep farmer. After a PhD on the Troubles in Northern Ireland she accepted a job at the newly opened Murdoch University in Western Australia to teach peace and conflict studies/social and political theory and explore her Australian family connections. She is the author of books about Northern Ireland, gender equity, and *Working Life: Arguments about Work in Australian Society*. In between she wrote about gardening. Four decades later, after trying Fremantle, Adelaide, Melbourne, Perth and the Otways, with too many renovations and building projects, she has built a multi-generational compound in Melbourne.

Belinda Probert

Imaginative Possession:
Learning to Live in
the Antipodes

First published in Australia in 2021
by Upswell Publishing
Perth, Western Australia
www.upswellpublishing.com

This book is copyright. Apart from any fair dealing for the purpose of private study, research, criticism or review, as permitted under the *Copyright Act 1968*, no part may be reproduced by any process without written permission. Enquiries should be made to the publisher.

Copyright © 2021 by Belinda Probert

The moral right of the author has been asserted.

ISBN: 978-0-6450763-0-51

 A catalogue record for this book is available from the National Library of Australia

Cover design by Peter Long
Cover image: Albert Koetsier X-ray/Science Photo Library
Typeset by Lasertype
Printed by McPherson's Printing Group

It can do no harm to settle on the public mind a deeper and more honest knowledge of the land than anything that myth and platitude allow, or to encourage love to over-run indifference.

Don Watson, *The Bush*

Contents

Chapter 1
Not feeling quite at home 1

Chapter 2
Reading about Australian landscapes 17

Chapter 3
Fear the hose: gardening my way into Australia 31

Chapter 4
Driving across the continent 41

Chapter 5
Living in the country and learning about the wildlife 51

Chapter 6
Learning about eucalypts 85

Chapter 7
The road out of the city 99

Chapter 8
Enlarging my horizons to the west 107

Chapter 9
Belonging in an immigrant nation 133

Chapter 10
Where I am 145

Notes 161

Acknowledgements 171

Chapter 1
Not feeling quite at home

In November 2011, on my 62nd birthday, I made an offer on a house and 28 acres of land in the Otways, an area of rolling hills and narrow valleys running down the coast inland from the Great Ocean Road in south-western Victoria. A week earlier I had been in London for two days, being interviewed for two jobs – Provost at Nazabayev University in Kazakhstan and Vice-Provost at University College London (UCL). Kazakhstan seemed by far the more interesting option but, on reflection, a little extreme. As for UCL, despite there being only two people on the short list and much nodding and winking about the job being mine before I got on the plane, I was rejected. The informal feedback that I managed to extract suggested that I was a bit too Australian for the all-male, all-internal appointment committee. I like to think this translates as my being insufficiently deferential, and sounding like a potentially loose cannon. That judgement was probably fair enough. If they had been fully informed they might have reasonably concluded that someone who was seriously considering a posting to Kazakhstan, a small farm in rural Victoria, and a posh place like UCL – all in the same week – was indeed likely to be unreliable.

My reaction to the feedback was contradictory. I bristled at the suggestion that I might be 'too Australian'. I grew up in Kent, went to school in Kent, and then to UCL as an undergraduate back in the late 1960s. Where was their loyalty to one of their own? But at the same time I felt pleased to have been spotted as someone who might behave like an Australian, which I self-servingly defined as being direct, unimpressed by status and with a laconic style.

Moving to Perth from London in the mid-1970s, aged twenty-six, to take a job at the newly opened Murdoch University was an intense liberation from what I felt were the oppressive class niceties of life in south-east England. I had no idea what Perth was like, or how far it was from Melbourne or Sydney, though I should have been alerted to the distances involved when I was informed that my contract would include one flight a year to the eastern states, with no purpose needing to be specified. However,  I had fearless Australian blood in me, with a maternal grandmother born in Tasmania in 1884 who went on to work with and then lead the Associated Country Women of the World (ACWW) from Bloomsbury. She had left Australia permanently in the early 1920s as a war widow so that her two young daughters could grow up close to their English father's family. I have no recollection of her ever talking about Australia to us, as she seemed single-mindedly focused on empowering rural women in the developing world. During my childhood she was far more likely to appear with an ACWW colleague from Sri Lanka or Kenya than any relative from Australia.

Mrs Charles Russell, as she insisted on being addressed for the sixty years of her widowhood, had no grandmotherly instincts at all, and only minimal motherly ones, perhaps because her own mother died when she was very young. Aged ninety she made her last visit to

MRS. CHARLES RUSSELL Lilla Russell with others represented us at the very first NGO meeting at Lake Success in 1947, and from then on for many years at each NGO Conference and meeting of the NGO Committee (later the Bureau), becoming its vice-chairman in 1950 and again in 1953. From 1953-9 she was also Chairman of our UN Standing Committee, of which she is still a valued member and 'elder statesman'.

"THEY bring out the red carpet at United Nations when Mrs. Russell comes", said a representative at UN in New York. That does not surprise me, I have never met anyone with such profound knowledge of UN Specialised Agencies and the Non-Governmental Organisations. If ACWW is able to make a considerable contribution to the work of the NGO's, it is largely due to Mrs. Russell.

Australia as honoured guest of the ACWW gathering in Perth in 1974, just two years before I arrived there. She was hard to know but much later I felt an immediate flash of recognition when I began reading Frank Moorhouse's description of Edith Campbell Berry starting her new life at the League of Nations in Geneva, in his novel *Grand Days*.[1] My grandmother, like Edith, spent her twenties in Sydney and was an equally passionate supporter of movements for world peace, talking to housewives' groups in Sydney and Tasmania about its importance, and going on to represent ACWW at the founding of the United Nations in San Francisco. While she rarely looked back at her Australian origins, my brothers and I knew we had a little bit of Australia in us. Having just finished a PhD on a topic that did not seem to suggest any obvious career path (the Troubles in Northern Ireland), I saw a paid relocation to Perth as an opportunity to find out more about this bit of my family history.

I arrived on a flight from London via Bombay in February 1976, seriously over-dressed for the walk across the melting tarmac to the Perth terminal. I squeezed my eyes as far as I could to protect them from the blinding afternoon sun while avoiding falling down the stair ramp, and for the next few days went around in wonderment at the intensity of the blue in the sky. By the time I left Perth three years later I was so sick of blue sky that I longed for Yorkshire, where I had sat in a damp farmhouse under the clouds writing my PhD. But in Perth I learned that if you said you wanted to do something, it seemed to be possible. I was no longer a minuscule piece of the English class system but an agent in my own life in a city full of possibilities for new immigrants. It was perhaps a small pond after London, but I had never felt like even a medium-sized fish before. No one asked me where I went to school, or even where I was from, or why I was there. As a young white woman from England what I said or did seemed to be taken at face value most of the time. I liked it a lot and started to be increasingly undeferential.

While Perth and Murdoch University were liberating in profound ways, there were aspects of life there in the 70s which were disconcerting for my very un-hippyish self. There were, for example, a lot of Orange People with their inexplicable enthusiasm for Bhagwan Shree Rajneesh. This even reached into academia, with the Dean of the School of Human Communication changing his name to Swami Anand Haridas, and overnight cutting the legs off his deanly jarrah desk so he could sit on a cushion beside it, in faded orange garments.

I recently read that Fremantle, where I had chosen to live, became a major hub for the movement, with hundreds of mostly young and university-educated people 'flocking to the port city to expand their religious dimensions through sex'.[2] Somehow I never noticed all the sex, but the famous Fremantle Market was full of rainbow-coloured beanies and crystals, in a haze of patchouli and incense sticks.

Newly made friends who had arrived from the radical left in Melbourne explained Perth's enthusiasm for cultish things over political involvement as the result of a 'lack of antibodies in the West'. After a couple of years in Australia I came to think that Melbourne probably had the perfect mix of egalitarianism, cloud cover and intellectual antibodies and that I should try to live there before returning to England. I made it across the Nullarbor in 1981, after a year in Adelaide on the way, and felt almost instantly at home.

There was a moment in my early thirties when I nearly went back to England. A position came up at the newly established Australian Studies Centre in London (now the Menzies Centre for Australian Studies), which was then located just round the corner from the flat where my Australian grandmother had lived from the moment her daughters left for university in the mid-1930s until her death in 1977. As I recall it, I told myself that I could either use this as a way to return home with a job or, alternatively, if I was unsuccessful I could have a baby. After all, I had bought a charming if decrepit house, and had a good, secure university job, with what seemed an amazing bonus at the time – three months paid maternity leave. I got an interview, by phone, which just goes to show that either not many people saw it as an interesting job, or I was managing to present myself plausibly as someone who now knew something about Australia. I had taught myself enough to teach undergraduate courses with titles like Political Economy of Australia, even if I was often only a few steps ahead of my students.

When I didn't get the job, I went for the baby option, and as soon as she arrived it occurred to me that I should perhaps formalise my status as an Australian. I might want to enter politics, or at the very least vote. I received a wattle tree seedling and certificate at Kew Library in 1985.

Melbourne is surely the most European of Australian cities – the place European immigrants are most likely to feel at home. This is in no small part because it lacks a dramatic setting which might regularly remind you that you are not, in fact, in Europe. There is no geographic drama like the Swan River and Kings Park in Perth, or Sydney Harbour, to constantly surprise you. Nor does the sun shine so much that you know it can't be England. The major avenues are lined with imposing elm trees that present the seasons in intensely familiar ways, and the ubiquitous plane trees in the inner city could remind you of Paris. The Royal Botanic Gardens (RBG) look in upon themselves, unlike Kings Park, which gazes out over the Swan River, or the Sydney Botanic Gardens with their prime position between the Opera House and Mrs Macquarie's Chair. The Melbourne gardens are designed around the eighteenth-century English landscape traditions established by William Kent, Humphry Repton and Capability Brown, with sweeping lawns leading you down to a system of lakes, surrounded by palms and camphor laurels and other tropical and subtropical plants.

When botanist and landscape designer William Guilfoyle arrived to take over the RBG in 1873 he was 'greatly surprised to find that one of the chief defects was an almost total absence ... of such flowering shrubs as camellias, azaleas, rhododendrons etc ... which every lover of flowers must admit are essential'.[3] As he set about his reorganisation of the gardens, moving exotic plants like the gardenia into pride of place, he explained that 'they had been quite overshadowed by useless indigenous scrub such as acacias and leptospermum – hakeas, eucalypts and melaleuca'.[4] One hundred years later, there was still only a tiny part of the Gardens devoted to Australian plants, and the most exciting new development after I arrived was the establishment of a splendid perennial border in 1986, which was further extended in the 1990s.[5] In Fremantle I had glimpsed the possibility of using Australian plants in the garden and in landscaping, but in Melbourne I sank easily back into quintessentially English forms of gardening, and the wattle tree died from neglect.

It was not hard for an Englishwoman to feel at home in Melbourne, and I was also perhaps too young still to appreciate the significance of my rather casual migration to Australia. Three decades later I immediately recognised and understood literary critic James Wood's reflections on the unintended consequences of his own similarly casual migration, from England to America. He knows what he has gained, but he 'had so little concept of what might be lost':

> 'Losing a country', or 'losing a home', if I gave the matter much thought when I was young, was an acute world-historical event, forcibly meted out on the victim, lamented and canonised in literature and theory as 'exile' or 'displacement', and defined with appropriate terminality by Edward Said in his essay 'Reflections on Exile'.[6]

None of this bears any relationship to Wood's relatively mundane experience, or mine. But for him, 'there is always the reality of a certain outsider-dom'.

***

For many years young children, a full-time job and a preoccupation with the intrinsically international movement for nuclear disarmament pushed any questions about where I belonged into the background. It was something of a surprise when I found myself wanting Australia to defeat the English cricket team. Next I became slightly defensive about my adopted country when outsiders criticised or patronised it. My loyalties were changing by osmosis, which my dictionary defines as 'a usually effortless often unconscious assimilation'.[7] There was no conscious decision to support the green and gold. It just happened.

I was obliged to think more consciously about my feelings when, in 1999, journalist and writer Donald Horne asked me to prepare a lecture on 'Class in Australia' as part of the centenary of Federation celebrations. The public lecture was one of ten to be delivered around the nation in early 2001, reflecting on 'the different forms of diversity and the sources of unity that have shaped, and continue to shape, Australian society'.[8] Class analysis was an integral element of any self-respecting social scientist's bag of tools in those more radical days, but this context seemed to ask for a more personal engagement with the topic.

I needed to expose the growing inequalities that the newly dominant neo-liberal ideas now shaping federal politics were bringing with them, but I also wanted to admit to my personal experience of 'egalitarianism' in this country (primarily a matter of manners), and my admiration for the Australian system of industrial arbitration and the historic concept of a fair and reasonable wage. In particular I admired the way a massive program of immigration after the Second World War had not led to the formation of an economic underclass. Immigrants might do 'dirty work' in factories, but they belonged to unions, were paid the same as anyone else, and earned enough to buy their own homes. I loved the fact that nobody tipped and nobody needed to be tipped.[9]

Much of what I had come to appreciate about Australian social and political history was in fact beginning to unravel under the pressure of neo-liberalism, but celebrating the centenary of Federation by writing about class in 2001 made me find words to explain why I had so happily become Australian – not just having Australian children and taking out citizenship, but really caring about the country.

From time to time all immigrants are surely asked what they miss about the country they came from. Within a few years of my move to Australia all my immediate family had left England too. My parents moved to France and lived for over twenty years in the foothills of the Pyrénées; my younger brother and his family also moved to France, to farm; and my older brother moved to New York. So there was never any family to go back to or rejoin, though close friends meant I regularly stopped over in London or Oxford en route to see my parents in France. Paradoxically it was friends I made while at Murdoch University in the 1970s who became my closest friends in England – friends who had ended up migrating in the opposite direction. I didn't miss stockbroker-belt Kent, where I had spent my childhood, or London itself, where I had studied. However, as James Wood says about his own experience, the loss can take a long time to make itself felt:

> What is peculiar, even a little bitter, about living for so many years away from the country of my birth is the slow revelation that I made a large choice many years ago that did not resemble a large choice at the time; that it has taken years for me to see this; and that this process of retrospective comprehension in fact constitutes a life – is indeed how life is lived.[10]

When my children were young Melbourne could hardly have been described as a cool city, and I don't recall ever seeing tourists except the ones waiting for a coach to take them to watch the Penguin Parade on Phillip Island. It was a political and cultural city, a city where ideas mattered, but it was also a city where the shops all closed at midday on Saturday (after closing at 5.30 p.m. on weekdays). There was not one café open after that time on Glenferrie Road in Hawthorn. The babyccino was yet to be imagined into being. It is amazing that we managed to get the shopping done at all, and it certainly ruined Saturday mornings for a decade or so, as we rushed from butcher to baker, from greengrocer to supermarket before the shutters came down.[11] But I also believed that people who worked in retail should enjoy weekends like everyone else, and preferred this to the unregulated American labour market where an underclass can provide anything, any time, but needs tips to survive.

As Melbourne began its transformation into the place that wins titles like 'the most liveable city in the world', it opened itself up on to the Yarra River, which runs through its centre, but it still remained a city looking in on itself. There are no ocean sunrises or sunsets to orient you. The tourists became younger and more global, attracted to the city's laneways, bars and music, even if they might also visit the penguins. On the streets of Fitzroy you are likely to hear Swedish or American accents, and internationalism became a taken-for-granted aspect of young professional identities. It became even easier to forget where Melbourne was located. The Indigenous history of the city is well hidden, and the garden state does a fine job disguising its underlying dryness. As the polymath George Seddon suggests, a 'confident metropolitan society is unlikely to value "sense of place", and will oppose the word "parochial" in contrast with their own metropolitan culture'.[12]

When asked what I miss about England, its cities have never come to mind. I think my answers over the decades have always related to the countryside, birdsong and the light. Images of the countryside and its colours surface effortlessly – the shape and colour of a mature horse chestnut tree in flower (not to mention collecting the biggest possible prickly seed pods for the game of conkers); the ancient beech forest at Toys Hill in Kent, where we would occasionally be taken to let off steam by running around the vast smooth grey tree trunks or somersaulting into piles of fallen leaves. That forest must have been genuinely magical as, just after I finished writing this down, I read Matthew Colloff's newly published book *Landscape of Our Hearts*, which proposes that landscape and history hold the key to Australian identity and national reconciliation. An ecologist who now lives in Canberra, he too grew up in Kent, and describes being taken to this same ancient woodland as a child. Like me he recalls 'exactly the smooth texture of the grey bark' and can still easily summon up 'the humic smell of the leaf litter in which we ran and rolled and laughed'. Understanding the power of such childhood experiences, he expresses the hope that 'children still go and play in that magical woodland'.[13] Sadly only a few of these memorable trees survived the great storm of 1987.

Later images that come easily to mind reflect my experience of the bare Yorkshire Dales near Bentham, where I sat in an old stone farmhouse writing up my PhD to the unforgettable sound of curlews outside my window; or a ploughed field in winter with the silhouettes of leafless oak trees; the light just before it snows; the light of long summer evenings. I would have missed these wherever I migrated to.

As I got to understand how big Western Australia was, and how few people lived there, I think I also at some level missed the extraordinary continuity of dense human habitation in England. Shortly before I left, I walked along the Ridgeway in Berkshire, which has been inhabited since prehistoric times, making it possible to imagine you are walking on the very same path that people have been walking along for 4000 years. It is not possible, in England, to imagine that you are the first person to be anywhere at all. In Australia it is not difficult to find such places. As I was flown around the Pilbara region of the continent in a tiny plane to meet students enrolled in Murdoch University's 'distance education' program, I gazed down in amazement at what was easy to read as a vast, largely uninhabited terrain between Tom Price and Newman, where only etiolated railway lines were visible as evidence of a human imprint.

It took much longer for me to understand that not only did I miss the English countryside, but that I did not feel at ease in the Australian countryside, even in the relatively tame parts. In fact, I didn't even know what to call non-urban Australia – the country? the bush? In classic Australian prosaic style the continent is administratively divided into metropolitan, rural and remote areas. Rural areas are defined as geographic areas that are located outside towns and cities, sometimes classified as the countryside. Remote areas are defined as places that are out of the way or 'considerably secluded from civilisation'. But then what is to count as 'bush'? The obvious person to answer this question for me is Don Watson, a quintessentially Australian writer who grew up on a small dairy farm near Poowong in Gippsland. After his biography of prime minister Paul Keating, and his book about the America he discovered as he criss-crossed that continent by rail listening to other passengers, Watson then turned his attention to the vast and varied inland that he and so many other writers believe still shapes what it means to be Australian. In his inestimable book, *The Bush*, he has to wrestle with its definition. His conclusion legitimises my confusion. It now connotes 'any one of many different kinds of forest, scrub, woodland, savannah, grassland and desert, made up of countless species in countless combinations of shape, colour, light and atmosphere so ephemeral and various that, unable to cope with them, our collective imagination has rendered all as bush, and often reduced it to a river red gum combined with a flock of sheep'.[14]

Whatever I was to call it, I came to see that I did not feel at home in the world just outside Melbourne. While it is easy to love the coast and the mountains or high hills of Victoria, I found it less easy to love the rest of the countryside, much as I wished to. It is not straightforward trying to put my finger on exactly why this mattered to me, why it unsettled my sense of comfort about becoming Australian. Was it because this identity felt slightly precarious when confronted with the unfamiliarity of the land – land where I was missing the literary and historical layers of association that I could find in the landscapes of my childhood? Was it also a reflection of the much wider unease about the interior of this continent expressed by many Australian-born writers? Or was it something more prosaic, like my childhood love of rural life, which I had somehow not been able to reproduce in Australia?

Then again, perhaps I just miss the prettiness of so much of the English and French countryside. A lot of rural Victoria seemed downright ugly to me. I let myself think this unkind thought after a particular trip through the Yarra Valley. I was driving to the Healesville Sanctuary with young children and wine was not on my mind. But the spread of vineyards in the 1970s and 80s was dramatic, and suddenly I was confronted with delightful green slopes on either side of the road, covered in neat regimented rows of vines, each with a mildew-alerting rose at the end, all edged with straight lines of windbreak plantings. The vista was beautiful and familiar. I was clearly one of those people whom Don Watson describes as finding the pangs of transplantation to the other side of the world 'less painful when sheep or vines were in sight'.[15] Vineyards create my kind of landscape, and today parts of the Yarra Valley feel positively French, or Italian.

I failed to make friends with anyone who actually lived in the country until I was in my fifties, so my experience of it, apart from beach holidays, was largely one of driving through it. In my early days in both Perth and Melbourne I would constantly ask people to tell me the name of that tree over there, or this flowering shrub that was clearly indigenous. What I soon realised was that nearly everyone could tell a gum tree from a wattle or a bottle brush, but that was about as far as it went. I am sure I looked down on this widespread inability to tell one eucalypt from another – until I set about the explicit task of learning to tell the difference for myself. As I explain later, I learned to eat humble pie. For now, to my untutored eye, what may well have been native grasslands just looked like neglected paddocks as I drove down the freeway to Geelong.

After thirty years of living in Melbourne, where there is nearly always a cloud somewhere in the sky, I needed a new job and was free to look around the continent, or at least to any town or city that had a university. The point of leaving Melbourne was, in no small part, to move somewhere that would not let me forget I was in Australia. Darwin and Perth came out on top when other criteria were added, even though friends were incredulous that I was considering Darwin (just as later they rolled their eyes about Kazakhstan). Luckily for me, the University of Western Australia kindly came up with a good-looking opportunity. As I flew over for the interview the sky was as blue as ever, the sun was still setting over the Indian Ocean, and Kings Park and the Swan River beckoned.

Living again in the west, in Perth this time rather than Fremantle, had the desired effect on my consciousness. I had successfully destabilised my own sense of being Australian, making it impossible to ignore the wider country and its sometime strangeness. The resources boom, then in full swing, was a reminder of how Western Australia's development has been shaped by periodic waves of investment and immigration. Each wave has seemed to erase the previous physical patterns of accommodation to the environment, and this time the city and the mining regions echoed with new British accents. It was a stark reminder of the youthfulness of the Australian nation, something which is somehow less remarkable in the rather staid, gold-rush grandeur of Melbourne's city streets.

I noticed that in Perth Australia Day seemed to be celebrated with far greater enthusiasm than I had ever noticed in Melbourne. Prime Minister John Howard's Australia Day address in 2005 attempted to define our cultural and political distinctiveness in terms of our British and Irish 'origins', and as we discovered later, he was working on a new citizenship test that would require everyone to know that Donald Bradman was a cricketer while Walter Lindrum and Hubert Oppenheimer were not. Less than twenty years later it is hard to take this question seriously. But instead of bristling at this Australia Day address, as I most certainly would have done in Melbourne, I found myself thinking about our continued inability to understand the country's unique physical environment. In Perth it is hard not to notice that this youthful nation inhabits an ancient continent unlike any other – a natural environment that helps define Australia, even for those who may well feel uncomfortable in it.

My thinking about this would have been largely unproductive had not George Seddon, a Fremantle resident, just published what he called his 'last and final book', *The Old Country: Landscapes, Plants and People*. In this he confronts the ways we do not feel 'at home' as Australians and asks how we might come to feel more so. It was Seddon who assured me that my feelings did not signify some inadequacy on my part, and that they might even be worth examining more closely. At the same time he provided a rich, multi-disciplinary framework for thinking about how and why Australia's immigrants have been unable to fully grasp the peculiarities of the continent. The problem was more profound than I had imagined. It was not just a question of botanical or geological ignorance. As Seddon puts it:

> The enduring form of possession is imaginative possession, which is fed by knowledge, understanding, associations, stories and images, affections and, finally incorporation of the environment into the self, until it becomes part of our sense of personal identity.[16]

The challenge to any imaginative possession of Australia is greatly heightened by several of its peculiarities. The continent is both staggeringly old (rocks in the Pilbara have now been dated to over 3.5 billion years ago), and also, in important respects, very young having broken free from Antarctica a mere sixty million years ago. It is also the only continent that has travelled almost from the pole to the equator, from south to north, and it is still on the move. Its migrating humans have always come in the opposite direction, from the north or north-west. On arrival they encounter plants that have come from the south, and before that the east and the west, and a physical place that is nothing like any of their homelands:

> ... not the Indonesian archipelago, not Britain, Ireland, southern Europe, not southern China nor India nor Vietnam. Its biorhythms are remote from any of the lands to the north, and they have been hard to learn.[17]

Thirty years earlier Seddon had pointed out that we know very little about the evolution of Australians' perceptual attitudes to our unique environment. He reminds us that by the early 1970s there were over 100 000 people of Greek origin living in Melbourne, and we know a lot about the work they did and where they lived and how they voted. But what did they make of the Victorian countryside?[18]

I found it rather encouraging to discover that I was in good company in my inability to understand the landscapes through which I had been driving. I learned that even though Donald Horne grew up in rural Muswellbrook in the Upper Hunter region of New South Wales, it was not until he moved to Sydney as a university student that he learned anything much about nature. Similarly, the eminent historian Keith Hancock, who went on to write one of the great Australian environmental histories (of the Monaro region) revealed that, although he grew up in rural Gippsland at the beginning of the twentieth century, he had no one to help him 'read the story which time had written upon Australian earth ... My teachers could not help me to use my eyes, because nobody had helped them to use their eyes'. [19] He wondered if things are different today in Gippsland.

Half a century later Don Watson was growing up in rural Gippsland, and nothing seems to have changed. Like Horne and Hancock, Watson was in his twenties before he saw 'the bush'. Fishing took him along the streams of the Great Dividing Range:

> I had to go camping to hear what my ancestors had heard in the mornings: the cacophony when every bird seems determined to tell all the others that it has survived the night. I saw my first lyrebird this way, first bowerbird and whipbird, first wombat and first dingo. It was the first time I heard the silence creep over the land as the day got older, and the first and only time I was chased by a tiger snake.[20]

The difficulties of comprehension experienced by successive waves of immigrants to the continent were not confined to the unfamiliar nature of its geology and flora and fauna. The landscape was rapidly being transformed by the newcomers, and we now know that Australian agriculture as practised by mostly English and Scottish settlers was devastating in its impact on the environment. George Seddon himself, growing up in the Wimmera, found no one who could tell him about the plants or birds or geology or even the history of settlement where he lived. He never saw a marsupial in its natural setting apart from possums, and there was no natural vegetation left. 'There was no Walden Pond at Horsham or Nhil, and could have been no Thoreau or Gilbert White or even Huck Finn'.[21] The landscape of his youth had been radically impoverished, and was now dominated by wheat paddocks, plantations of sugar gums from South Australia, weeds and a limited range of exotic imports. The only animals Seddon knew were dogs, cats, rabbits, horses, sheep and cows. The reference to Gilbert White's *The Natural History of Selborne* strikes a personal chord. First published in 1789, this book has been continuously in print ever since, which is surely remarkable for a book about the flora and fauna of eighteenth-century England. It was one of my mother's favourite books, which may explain something about the things I find I need to know. Or not. I have her father's 'new edition' (the second of 300 editions), published in 1880, in which he has noted that he received it as a student at Loretto School in Scotland, in 1886.

While it was reassuring to know that I was far from alone in finding the landscape hard to understand, let alone love, I also realised that this could not be fixed simply by learning more about the geology, plants and animals of the continent. If I wanted to feel at home, and even become fully Australian, there was other work to be done. The bush is, as Watson insists, both real and imaginary. And for Seddon 'the imaginative apprehension of a continent is as much a pioneering enterprise as breaking the clod'.[22] But where to start my imaginative apprehension?

Chapter 2
Reading about Australian landscapes

I needed writers to help me recognise and clarify my vague sense of unease in the Australian landscape. Without Australian writers and their novels, memoirs and environmental histories I would understand a great deal less about my life in the Antipodes. A few, like George Seddon, have produced veritable light-bulb moments. It is true that I am the kind of person who has bought far too many books, some of which I may never read, simply because a book seems the logical place to start when I feel a need to understand something. Perhaps not surprisingly I have thought about a reading list that could be handed to every new Australian, along with their certificate of citizenship. I would like them to be given a tiny wattle plant as well, but I fear that horse has bolted, along with Wattle Day. The reading list is intended to help us develop a sense of place, and to assist with our 'imaginative apprehension' of the continent. I began asking friends and colleagues what they thought could be on such a list, but most said they'd 'have to think about it'. My approach to the list is neither rigorous nor scholarly – more shopping list than annotated bibliography – and I don't doubt that things which I have found enlightening or stimulating would not appeal to everyone. I confess I am puzzled that so much of the landscape writing that has helped me is written by men. But many kinds of writing can surely play a role, including Indigenous writing, crime writing,[23] gardening books, natural history, children's books, memoirs, literary novels and poetry, as well as the newer field of environmental history. For those of us who arrived after 1788, books can do a lot to help us imaginatively possess the Australian landscape.

When I arrived at the newly opened Murdoch University in 1976, I pestered my Australian-born colleagues to give me their version of a reading list for immigrants. I was profoundly ignorant. I couldn't understand why everyone seemed to be so politically shell-shocked, as the recent sacking of the Whitlam Government had not attracted my attention in England. I was offered a lot of political history and social realism, and most of it reflected the increasingly urban character of Australian lives; where the natural environment made an appearance it was often as a place of fear or alienation. Yet of all the introductory reading I got through in my short first time living in the west, the books I remember most clearly now are those which somehow brought the physical landscape to life. The works that surface first, four decades after I read them, include Katharine Susannah Prichard's *Coonardoo*, Patrick White's *Tree of Man* and Henry Handel Richardson's *The Fortunes of Richard Mahony*.

Since moving to Victoria I have come to understand quite a lot about the nature of bushfires, and seen many hours of dramatic TV coverage, but I can still feel the heat and overwhelming fury of the fire that threatened Stan Parker in *Tree of Man*. What made this novel memorable was not the universal human themes which made it such a success in the literary world, but the particularity of that patch of 'scrub' and its vulnerability to fire. I could feel the fire that Stan faced – decades before I came close to the real thing in Victoria. 'There was a smoking, and smarting, and crackling, and breaking, and crashing. The fire was reaching upward from the undergrowth, and higher upward, to embrace whole trees. There was a sighing of sap.'[24]

Equally searing for someone who had grown up in the Weald of Kent was Jill Ker Conway's memoir, *The Road from Coorain*, which I read a decade later in Melbourne, gripped by her account of the devastating drought that persisted through the early 1940s, destroying her family's life on the Western Plains of New South Wales. Describing the vast tract of land her father was granted as a soldier settler in 1929, she observes that 'the scale of each holding was beyond European dreams of avarice. Each settler could look out to the vacant horizon knowing that all he saw was his'.[25] Conway's description of the plants and animals that have evolved on the plains evokes a world that is profoundly unfamiliar to European sensibilities, set in a landscape of flat enormity. 'Human purposes are dwarfed by such a blank horizon ... On the plains, the horizon is always with us and there is no retreating from it. Its blankness travels with our every step and waits for us at every point of the compass.'[26]

Most Australians, let alone those migrating from Europe, might find such a landscape intimidating or uninteresting or even boring, for what grows or lives there tends to hug the ground, or disappear into the blue-grey, silver, yellow, gold and red clay colours that predominate. As Conway describes it, the 'creatures that inhabit this earth carry its colours in their feathers, fur or scales'. Born into this landscape, she shared with her father a profound sense of connection to it:

> Here, pressed into the earth by the weight of that enormous sky, there is real peace. To those who know it, the annihilation of the self, subsumed into the vast emptiness of nature, is akin to a religious experience ... What was social and sensory deprivation for the stranger was the earth and sky that made us what we were.[27]

By the time this memoir was published I had driven across the Nullarbor Plain twice – travelling from Perth to Melbourne and back in an old Holden panel van with the requisite mattress in the back, and sleeping out under a sky of such vastness that I was ready for Conway's descriptions. And I had read Eric Rolls' depiction of the plains around Bathurst where 'as far as the horizon there is no rise, no dip. The plains are like flat, black ocean'.[28]

But it wasn't Conway's skies or horizons that I remembered without difficulty thirty years later, but rather her account of the five years when it did not rain. Thirty-two thousand acres of carefully managed grazing property could not withstand more than three years without rain. 'As the winds seared our land, they took away the dry herbage, piled it against the fences, and then slowly began to silt over the debris.'[29] Her description of the inevitable dust storms is as unforgettable as Patrick White's description of the bushfire threatening Stan Parker.

Conway writes with an acute understanding of the evolution of indigenous fauna, treading on the fragile habitat with padded paws and claws which left the roots of grass intact. She knows these grasses had never been cropped by ruminant animals until the settlers arrived, and that her family's starving sheep and cattle tore up roots to eat, loosening the top soil with their sharp hooves, and devastating that ancient ecology.[30] But it is the personal story of her family's losses that stayed with me rather than the environmental destruction.

After Conway I felt no need to read more about the human experience of drought on the land. I don't think that I took in her relatively brief comments about the sharpness of sheep's hooves and the devastating impact of ruminant animals. A couple of years after her memoir was published I was invited to attend a celebration in Barcaldine, Queensland, to mark the centenary of the great Shearers' Strike and the beginnings of the Australian Labor Party. I was much more interested in the industrial relations underpinning the wool industry and the strength of Australian labour politics than the fragility of Australian soil and the industry's sustainability. I would have been better informed if I had read Tim Flannery's somewhat controversial *The Future Eaters* when it came out, but I wasn't disposed to be interested in geology and fragile soils. Nothing in my English background prepared me for the idea that sheep could be dangerous. I spent my teenage weekends working on a sheep farm beside the Brands Hatch motor racing circuit, owned by a very eccentric man who specialised in rare breeds, including some which needed to wear leather boots in the wet fields of Kent. After twenty years in Australia I was still hoping to meet someone with what I would call a sheep farm. I was not at all ready to consider the possibility that sheep might have been a big mistake.

It was not long after I moved to Melbourne that fire – as an intrinsic element of Australian life – ceased to be a purely literary experience. On an extremely hot February day in 1983, a group of us had gone into the city to see a movie in some air-conditioned comfort. When we emerged into the late evening we all noticed an unusual smokey smell in the air, but it took the radio to tell us what was burning when we got home. I find our unfamiliarity hard to believe now. The Ash Wednesday bushfires were the worst in Australian history until Black Saturday, killing seventy-five people and destroying over 3000 buildings. In Upper Beaconsfield, less than an hour's drive from the cinema, twenty-one people died.

Thirty years later, only three years after Black Saturday in 2009, I bought my bit of land in the Otways, ignorant of the fact that the Ash Wednesday fires had come within a hundred yards of my new front door. As the first summer came around my new neighbours insisted that I have a fire plan and that I tell them what it was. I downloaded a lot of advice from the Country Fire Authority website, but essentially accepted that I should always leave early on any day of serious fire risk. This was the period when the policy of 'Prepare, Stay and Defend or Leave Early', commonly called 'Stay or Go', came under critical scrutiny for its role in the Black Saturday deaths. Before my second summer in the country Robert Kenny's 'investigative memoir' *Gardens of Fire* was published. I might not have noticed it had he not previously written a rather remarkable book called *The Lamb Enters the Dreaming*, which I had bought, thinking I *should* read it. It traces the life of Nathanael Pepper of the Wotjobaluk people, who was born just as the first pastoralists were driving cattle and sheep into Victoria's Wimmera region. Behind the pastoralists came Christian missionaries, who were critical of the settlers' violence, but also hostile to the traditional beliefs of Aboriginal people. Pepper converted to Christianity in 1860.

I hadn't read the book then, but it was on my list of self-improving books (many of which remain unread for ever). In *Gardens of Fire* Kenny is writing about his own experience of being burnt out on Black Saturday – by a grass fire that found his modest house and library near Redesdale, about 120 kilometres north of Melbourne. On 7 February 2009 Kenny was at home, in a house made of wood and asbestos cement sheeting sitting on a natural terrace about two-thirds up the slope of a ridge. This is in pastoral country, with what he describes as 'only thin, short grass after more than a decade of drought. There are no longer cattle on it because there is nothing for them to eat. Surely no real danger'.[31] He had been pleased to find a place to buy that wasn't too wooded, and where any grass would be kept down by cattle.

I am reading about this while sitting in my timber house, located near the top of a small ridge that marks the beginning of the Otway hills between Deans Marsh and Aireys Inlet. I, too, was pleased to find a property that was not too wooded, surrounded by small paddocks where Belted Galloways and a small herd of Herefords kept the grass under control and provided several of us along the ridge with an annual freezer full of beef. The one real danger would always be a grass fire, racing from the little treed creek at the bottom of my property, up the hill across a couple of paddocks and to the edge of my garden. My fire plan is still to leave early on any day defined as Extreme Fire Danger or worse, even though I am instinctively drawn to the challenge of 'stay and defend', thinking of myself as practical, sensible and resourceful. My more experienced neighbours who all have stay and defend plans like to know where I will be, and occasionally raise an eyebrow when I am slow to depart. Five years later I would approach fire risk differently, but I am still really new to this.

Robert Kenny helped me fully imagine what the experience of fire might be like.

There are many clear warnings about the weather conditions all through that week, predicted to be among the worst ever recorded and worse than Ash Wednesday, so all of Victoria is apprehensive. In the late morning the temperature rises and so does the wind. I stay inside in Fitzroy. Kenny is well prepared, with a fire pump, long fire hose, the right clothes and boots always by his back door and lots of water in his steel and concrete tanks. His decision to stay and defend is not unwise, as a grass fire is the worst threat his property faces. By midday, he tells us, 'the sky starts to silt over. I hope it is high cloud, the harbinger of a cool change. But, outside, I know such thoughts are a fool's consolation. I can smell it is high smoke. Smoke from a distant fire'.[32]

In mid-afternoon Kenny goes outside again and sees not just the high distant smoke, but other smoke, 'a too distinct huge column, darkly billowing up from behind the back ridge of my property, to the north-west, one or two kilometres away, directly upwind from my house'.[33] And then the fire reaches him, even though the tree canopies have not caught alight and the grass is only two or three centimetres high. The flame is moving so fast and so high that his fire hose does almost nothing to deter it. 'The fire's behaviour is wild, jumping from one thing to another. Embers whirl and tangle, dart up in the air, dive to the ground. They are tiny, no more than a square millimetre. Yet they manage to set alight anything flammable they touch – that is, anything organic'.[34]

He is driven inside when his pump dies (the petrol evaporating in the heat), but the house seems remarkably resilient even as 'red flames lap at the windows'. So much so, that eventually Kenny can venture outside as the front passes and start to extinguish spot fires with his buckets and water-soaked mop. This account of retreating inside while the fire front passes and then emerging to deal with the spot fires left behind can be found in the reports of many who have successfully stayed to defend. I already had my box of tennis balls to be soaked and placed at the top of my down pipes to allow the gutters to be filled with water on days of extreme fire danger, but after reading Kenny's account of the fire melting any plastic in his garden watering system, I went almost immediately to Bunnings in Colac to buy galvanised iron buckets (and brass tap fittings) to replace the plastic ones I had imagined using in extinguishing spot fires.

The most poignant moment in Kenny's memoir comes as he returns inside to look for his cat, beginning to feel 'optimistic that the house will be safe'. Wondering how smoke is getting into his house he looks up at the kitchen ceiling:

> Where there had been an exhaust fan is now a hole through which I see only roaring flame fuelled by the oregon pine structure. It will not be long before the ceiling collapses. Embers are already falling from the ceiling throughout the increasingly smoke-filled house.

The power of this moment is heightened dramatically by an interlude, inserted between the point where he realises the fire front has passed his house and he can safely go outside, and the point where he returns inside and looks up. In this interlude Kenny describes the origins of the dominant structural form taken by Australia's domestic buildings, which comes to us from innovations in house building on the American Midwest frontier during the 1830s. I read this part, sitting inside just such a house, on a site just like his. I become acutely aware of the wooden stumps lifting my house above the ground to provide stability and air circulation as well as an adequate horizontal platform for a house on a slope. Scrabbling around bent over under my house is something I do a lot, as the dam pump is located there and is regularly in need of attention, requiring me to turn it on and off in search of leaks, prime it and check pressure, like everyone else with a rural property dependent on dams and tank water. I know exactly where the bearers are laid across the stumps as I hit my head

on them from time to time when I am wrestling with the pump or need to turn off the power to the electric fencing (which for some strange reason is also located just under the floor next to the pump).

Having engaged in some minor renovation of my house, I could follow Kenny's description of the way wooden floor boards are laid and see my own light timber stud walls rising up from the bearers with their metal bracing – probably radiata pine as opposed to the oregon used in his house. As he points out, 'While the comparatively light timber pieces seem insubstantial in themselves, combined they form a strong and stable wall'.[35] Above the walls, ceiling joists are placed. 'If the room span is great, hanging beams are introduced, these are large pieces that lie at right angles across the top of the joists from wall to wall, to which the joists are attached, and therefore "hang".'[36] My renovations have involved removing a couple of internal walls to make a very large kitchen and living area and I know exactly where those hanging beams are located. Above the ceiling joists are the light timber frames for the roof, covered in timber battens to provide support for the roofing material, usually sheet metal, and in my case classic corrugated iron. Kenny writes that ceiling cavities provide air circulation, as well as providing 'particularly well designed living areas for a myriad of pests including mice, rats, wasps, possums, birds, snakes, even feral cats – anything that can get in and is looking for a secluded home close to the feast of human habitation'.[37] I can immediately visualise my own ceiling cavity. The vendor had warned me I should climb up there regularly to nail poison baits to the roof framing. It is a forest of timber above the ceiling. What had never occurred to me, despite my building knowledge, was that all 'this light timber and circulating air means the conventional Australian home is a perfect pyre'.[38]

After reading Kenny's memoir I looked at my country house in a new way. Wet tennis balls were not going to be enough. If I was ever going to stay and defend there were a lot of cracks that needed to be filled for I now knew that flying embers could be tiny enough to get through metal fly screens. The knowledge didn't make me think I couldn't or shouldn't ever stay and defend, just that I had a lot to do before it would be a safe option.

As it turns out I needed to read one more thing to put my bravado in proper perspective. Only a week after Black Saturday, the environmental historian Tom Griffiths had written a short piece bringing all his historical knowledge of Victoria's fires to bear on our ignorance about the environment in which we live. It opens this way:

> We should have seen this coming. We *did* see this coming. Yet we failed to save lives. We have still not lived long enough.[39]

He ends by insisting that 'lived experience alone, however vivid and traumatic, was never going to be enough to guide people in such circumstances'. In between he explains why this relatively cool corner of the continent is 'the most distinctive fire region of Australia and the most dangerous in the world'.

It had never occurred to me that Victoria would be more dangerous than hotter Australian states. But as Griffiths makes clear this is the result of the coming together of weather systems, topography and the predominance of ash-type eucalypts:

> When a high pressure system stalls in the Tasman Sea, hot northerly winds flow relentlessly down from central Australia across the densely vegetated south-east of the continent. This fiery 'flume' brews a deadly chemistry of air and fuel. The mountain topography of steep slopes, ridges and valleys

channel the hot air, temperatures climb to searing extremes, and humidity evaporates such that the air crackles. Lightning attacks the land ahead of the delayed cold front and a dramatic southerly change turns the raging fires suddenly upon its victims.

The ferocious nature of Victoria's fires is magnified dramatically by the way eucalypts in this corner of the continent have adapted to fire, over millions of years. Our mountain ash (*Eucalyptus regnans*) and alpine ash (*Eucalyptus delegatensis*) are dependent on their seeds to regenerate, unlike the eucalypts that have lignotubers from which new shoots can sprout when the tree is damaged by fire. (I have learned that they are called 'ash' trees despite being eucalypts because their timber is pale, strong and straight-grained like the unrelated ash (*Fraxinus*) found in the northern hemisphere.) The problem for eucalypt seeds is that they are housed in the toughest of casings; they are not called 'gumnuts' for nothing. They do not float to earth like sycamore seeds, nor plop down annually like acorns or conkers. I grew up trying to catch sycamore seeds as they helicoptered erratically to the ground, and cracking open the soft if prickly covering of the horse chestnut seed in order to create a playground weapon on a string, and turning acorns into eggs in egg cups. But you clearly needed pliers or a mallet to get into a gumnut. Or the ferocious heat of a bushfire to open it up and release the seed:

> These particularly grand and magnificent trees have evolved to commit mass suicide once every few hundred years – and in European times, more frequently ... These are wet mountain forests that only burn on rare days at the end of long droughts, after prolonged heatwaves, and when the flume is in full gear. And when they do burn, they do so with atomic power.

Learning this about mountain ash trees made me admire them more, after an unpromising initial relationship. On my first drives through the great mountain ash forests that surround Melbourne to the east, I found them both gloomy and boring. Now I realised that my reaction was not unreasonable, in some respects at least. Because of their habit of mass suicide and mass regeneration, mountain ash generally grow in even-aged and uniform stands. The trees all looked the same to me because they *are* in fact the same, growing so close together that nothing much else of substance gets a look in.

Not only did they all look the same at first view, but they looked pretty much the same whatever the time of year when we drove through them. I sympathised with Judge Barron Field's response on arriving from England in 1814 as the first Supreme Court Judge

in New South Wales. More than anything he loved the poetry of Wordsworth, so it is perhaps not surprising he 'deplored the monotony of the unchanging grey-green eucalypt forests that ringed him round in early Sydney'. As George Seddon tells us:

> He was raised to a different cycle, one of annual death and renewal, which is a founding myth of the western world: of Orpheus and Eurydice, of the Crucifixion and the Resurrection, of a death that brings life. He was missing more than an autumnal leaf fall. He mourned a metaphor, one that had shaped his culture.[40]

I have lived in Australia for forty-five years now, mostly in Victoria, and only in the past ten years have I begun to know or understand the trees around me. My emotional investment was initially in the grand avenues of elms to be found in Melbourne, long after the tree had been lost to the English countryside because of Dutch elm disease, a fungus which killed 20 million elm trees within twenty years. And I doubt I would have had enough incentive to read much about the evolutionary brilliance of the mountain ash, or any other scientific literature that might explain the natural world I find myself in, were it not for the debates about fire management that emerged after Ash Wednesday.

Tom Griffiths wrote four powerful pages immediately after Black Saturday which I have shared with friends and family here and overseas, and they have all reacted with some version of 'Ah! Now I begin to understand why you have been burning ...'. But he was also writing to save lives and his strongest words are reserved for the idea that 'staying and defending' is a sensible option for anyone without an underground bunker. His plea is that we move beyond 'an undifferentiated, colonial sense of "the bush" as an amorphous sameness with which we do battle, and instead empower local residents and their knowledge of local ecologies ... Clearing the backyard, cleaning the gutters and installing a better water pump cannot save an ordinary home in the path of a surging torrent of explosive gas in the fire flume'.

Chapter 3
Fear the hose: gardening my way into Australia

Making a garden clearly involves some engagement with the local natural environment, though it is also true that some great gardens are built to defy nature, bring water and green plants to arid zones, or involve moving hills and villages that spoil the view. I have spent an inordinate amount of my life gardening and have always imagined myself working with nature rather than against it. In either hemisphere I would certainly have gardened – and done a lot of it. Gardening is in my genes, on one side at least. My Australian grandmother chose to spend the second half of her life in a small flat at the top of an old apartment block just off Tottenham Court Road in London, called Bedford Court Mansions. She wanted to be in the thick of things as she devoted herself to the Associated Country Women of the World (ACWW), representing it anywhere she could get a foot in the door, from the United Nations to the Institute for Rural Life at Home and Overseas. There might have been a pot plant of some kind on her tiny kitchen balcony, but she had no personal enthusiasm for gardening or farming, only a life-long interest in ensuring women had access to fresh food. She began by organising a housewives' league to campaign for the creation of fruit and vegetable markets in Sydney's suburbs just after the First World War.

However, this grandmother, Lilla Williams, married into a very long line of gardeners. Travelling to England – 'home' – in 1914 with her father, to celebrate his retirement from a long and illustrious career with the Bank of Australasia, she had plenty of time to get to know the Englishman who boarded at Singapore, taking leave from his position as Principal of Patna College in the East Indian state of Bihar. The college features in E. M. Forster's novel *A Passage to India* as Chandrapore College, and my grandfather also appears in the character of Fielding. His gardening genes can be traced back to the sixteenth century, and his childhood had been spent in a garden already well known at the turn of the seventeenth century, and redesigned by Humphry Repton in the eighteenth century. Both his sisters were serious gardeners, and one of them married the editor of the *American Atlantic Monthly* after the Second World War, and inherited and then developed an admired garden in Massachusetts that was famous for its peonies. Charles Russell did not live long enough to test his Australian wife's adjustment to English country life, because despite surviving Gallipoli, he was killed fighting in Palestine in 1917. He left behind two very young babies, but both my mother and her sister inherited the Russell gardening genes, and my mother passed them on to me.

People who write about gardening often acknowledge the difference between 'doing some gardening' and 'making a garden', or between

'plantsmen and women' and 'garden landscapers'. A plantswoman is someone who cares deeply about individual plants and often prefers to have one of everything without much regard for how it all might look, as long as the plants thrive. The landscaper insists that you have should always have three or five of anything (not two or four), and is primarily interested in the overall design, which these days might include huge amounts of plant repetition. For the individual gardener with enough garden to 'design' there is still the question, nonetheless, of what kind of garden you are trying to create, and why. What are the feelings that you want your garden to induce?

From the beginning I have wanted to be in the business of 'making a garden' rather than 'doing some gardening', and I am well known among my gardening friends for ruthlessly pulling out and giving away healthy plants that don't fit in with my feelings. If you want to 'make a garden' as well as 'do some gardening' (and I do not see any moral distinction here), there are hundreds of books to advise you, full of tantalising pictures of other people's realised dreams as well as instructions on how to use graph paper. It is more difficult to find a writer who can help us use the principles of design to give shape to our own inarticulate desires. This is no easy task since a garden, as the writer Michael Pollan insists, is 'a *place*, and not just a collection of plants':

> A garden will move us to the extent it engages the imagination as well as the senses. Among other things, a garden is a passage somewhere else – to the personal and shared past its scents evoke, to the distant places to which its forms allude ... Another way of saying the same thing is that gardens are simultaneously real places and representations. They bring together in one place, nature and our ideas about nature.[41]

So apart from learning about new soils, new climate, new light (which did not strike me as intrinsically interesting problems for many years), I – like any other immigrant – had to think about the unexamined meaning of my gardening, and how it was going to translate to Australia. My problem was that I had Sissinghurst syndrome from my very early years. I grew up in Kent, played lacrosse in the same team with one of the daughters from Sissinghurst Farm, and was regularly taken as a child to visit large and stately gardens in the south-east of England. I can still see myself running up and down immaculate swathes of green grass between magnificently maintained perennial borders in Sir Frederick Stern's famous garden, Highdown, while my mother and my elderly Russell great-aunt from America engaged in earnest discussion with him about tree peonies and gardening on chalk.

The first garden I could call my own was in Fremantle, on pure sand. It was a period when the small minority of residents who were interested in using Australian plants were just as likely to go for a lemon-scented gum or two – behind a horizontal Mission Brown paling fence – as anything more suited to the suburbs. Not surprisingly I struggled to define an aesthetic in which I could use newly discovered Australian plants to create some faint echo of the Weald of Kent. In fact I struggled to grow anything at all. I began to learn something about the profoundly unfamiliar, dramatic, but often spikey Western Australian flowering plants without really being able to connect them to my instincts about 'making a garden'. For, in Michael Pollan's words, my desire to garden was, at least in part, 'an urge to recover a place remembered from childhood'.[42] This desire is of course common to immigrants from all countries, and it is not difficult to spot the Italian or Greek post-war suburbs in Melbourne from their gardens. But this need to affirm individual or cultural identity creates immigrant cities that are characterised by discordant landscapes. I still find it discomforting to see a glossy green-leaved camellia covered in carmine blossoms next to a wispy yellow-flowering wattle.

As I was wrestling with roses in sand, Seddon was writing his most influential book, *Sense of Place*, his response to the environment of the Swan Coastal Plain in Western Australia. A facsimile edition with two new introductory essays has just been published by UWAP in recognition of its enduring importance. The book is divided into three parts, covering the land including geological history, climate and soils; the plants and their evolutionary history; and finally 'man', the response of Aboriginal communities, the settlers and the designers of Perth and Fremantle. Seddon concludes the book saying that 'a sense of place shows most clearly in the way the community feels about and uses the landscape', noting the pleasures diverse communities in Perth find in different parts of the coastline, especially Rottnest and both ocean and river beaches. His final comment, however, felt as if it was aimed at me. 'A sense of place is least expressed in our gardening styles and landscape architecture. An indigenous landscape style has been slow to evolve ... Our gardening preferences are still English, and good Western Australian bush is dug up to plant roses'.[43] In his final book three decades later, George Seddon still thinks that contemporary suburban gardening is strongly influenced by imported cultural identity, and that 'most gardens reject the local environment'.[44] He urges us to 'fear the hose', and looks forward to the 'extinction of our new-found reticulation systems', which will lead to better gardens.

After four years of metaphorically and literally unproductive gardening in sand I arrived in Melbourne. I knew I had found a garden home, but mainly in the sense that the soils and climate made it possible to garden in almost any style. I could play with something Mediterranean, pursue my aesthetic (and cultivatory) struggles with Australian flora, or fall back into an extraordinarily fast-growing English country garden style. But as I criss-crossed the eastern suburbs between my home in Kew and work in Clayton I saw nothing distinctively Australian to inspire me. I defaulted into the perennial plant catalogues as I settled into this part of Australia often defined as 'favourable to gardening' – which Seddon skewers as meaning 'slightly more amenable to pursuing generally inappropriate goals than the rest of the country'.[45] My Melbourne life started twenty-five years before the Australian Garden at Cranbourne opened and the Royal Botanic Gardens seemed to be egging me on in my inappropriate habits by opening up that most splendid long, curved perennial bed, located where Government House can provide a fine colonial backdrop.[46] Here we were, still putting our colonial stamp on the land, ignoring its intrinsic attractions, and reproducing English landscapes and garden style.

In the late 1990s I was presented with an incentive to think more systematically about my increasingly ambivalent feelings regarding my garden 'practice'. I was asked if I would like to contribute a chapter to a book that the art critic and garden writer Peter Timms was editing, to be called *The Nature of Gardens*. It was not a gardening book, but a book about why we garden – the 'moral, social, philosophical and symbolic meanings behind this pastime that occupies so much of the free time of so many of us'.[47] Had I not migrated to a large multicultural city on the other side of the world, I might not really have understood the question. I would probably have continued to garden without really caring what it might 'mean'. But gardening in Australia made me increasingly aware that I did not understand what everyone else was doing in their gardens nor where their ideas came from, despite the ubiquity of the quarter-acre block. I had lost my childhood bearings but wasn't sure how to make myself at home in a Melbourne garden, yet alone in Australia.

I had been reviewing gardening books on radio with an impudence that now seems preposterous. Ramona Koval, the wonderful presenter of Radio National's *The Book Show*, had asked me if I would like to regularly discuss a book of my choosing on her program. She imagined, I think, that this segment would reflect areas of my professional expertise such as social policy, gender in the workplace and other worthy topics. I put to her instead that I should discuss books about gardening. Despite the fact that she knew nothing about gardening and cared even less, she agreed, and for several hilarious months we discussed large piles of new books about gardens, plants and gardening. I remember saying at some point, on air, that I did not care for the famous long driveway of lemon-scented gums that Dame Elizabeth Murdoch had planted on her property at Langwarrin. I think I said something about how these beautiful eucalypts, with their individual angles and forms, looked out of place in this particularly formal structure. There were a few phone calls to the ABC, but I survived.

Nothing I reviewed reflected much adjustment to the Australian environment or interest in what it might mean to us. And a quick glance at the gardening books section in any Australian bookshop in the 1990s revealed the perennial popularity of upper-class, English women authors, and some middle- or even working-class men who knew their pistils from their stamens, or their peduncles from their receptacles – though there were of course some creditable attempts to wean us off the English gentry's climatically inappropriate writings in favour of something more antipodean. At one point I mentioned, on air, the thrill of trying to make a blue poppy flower in Melbourne, which led to slap on the wrist from the late, great Tommy Garnett, who essentially accused me of being a foolish Englishwoman who had no idea where she was. Tommy Garnett was a gardening force to be reckoned with, having been an English and Australian headmaster (Geelong Grammar), horticulturist, ornithologist and author, not to mention the fact that he played first-class cricket for Somerset before the Second World War. We exchanged letters about this and he forgave me. This led to writing the odd gardening column for the *Saturday Age* on things like why salvias are so useful, or how to get a ripe tomato before Christmas. I was skating on thin ice giving advice though.

Despite this, the idea that the garden can provide us with an education – not just about how to grow plants – is particularly appealing to me. Not least because it is a source of pleasure for so many Australians. Survey data tells us that a very significant number of Australians 'absolutely love gardening, and nothing else competes', while more than half of us 'enjoy gardening'.[48] The crowds at the non-denominational Melbourne International Flower and Garden show or the Kings Park Festival of native plants each year are phenomenal, as are the queues at any plant sale. Both Michael Pollan and George Seddon showed me that you can write about the garden and be very funny and even caustic. Before reading them I found garden writing and garden television shows to be relentlessly enthusiastic and earnest as though every plant is wonderful, when clearly they are not. These writers also made me see that fine garden writing can do a lot to help with the imaginative possession of a place. Michael Pollan writes about the sites where nature and culture intersect – on our plates, in our farms and gardens and in our minds. He came to his understanding about the educational potential of gardening when he took on an old dairy farm in Connecticut. He describes what happened in a truly wonderful book called *Second Nature: A Gardener's Education:*

> I would not learn to garden very well before I'd learned about a few other things: about my proper place in nature ... about the somewhat peculiar attitudes toward the land that an American is born with; about the troubled borders between nature and culture; and about the experience of place, the moral implications of landscape design, and several other questions that the wish to harvest a few decent tomatoes had not prepared me for. It may be in my nature to complicate matters unduly, to search for large meanings in small things, but it seemed that there was a lot more going on in the garden than I'd expected to find.[49]

I had a chance to demonstrate that I had finally learned a thing or two when I returned to Western Australia for my second brief interlude in 2004 and bought a house in Subiaco. I discovered that in my long absence Kings Park had designed large areas devoted to developing the vocabulary of Perth gardeners, showing the public the extraordinary and showy array of native plants now available, displayed in contexts that many could aspire to. That year the Kings Park Festival laid out Australian flowers in designs that felt genuinely exciting, and it maintains this air of innovation and excitement every year. My new and empty garden took shape around large plantings of yellow kangaroo paws, which flourished in the sand.

By the time I returned to Melbourne (and a house with no garden to speak of, in Fitzroy), the Australian Garden in Cranbourne had begun to make its mark, providing the opportunity to 'get to know' – as their website quaintly puts it – 1700 different Australian plants, in explicitly uncompromising Australian landscapes.[50] Today it is a source of inspiration, information and as many opportunities to get educated as anyone could wish for.

In the same vein, the Victorian Open Gardens scheme had for years seemed to me to be mired in colonial Englishness – with the odd bush garden in Eltham thrown in for extreme contrast. Now the scheme introduced many of us to the paradigm-shifting garden created by Fiona Brockhoff in Sorrento, and her profoundly influential landscape design practice. In her garden the tensions between classical European forms (such as clipped hedges and box balls) and the looseness and irregularity of indigenous plants are resolved in glorious ways. There is no fetishising of 'native plants', only the evidence of learning to use what will thrive on a sand dune so close to the sea. This garden is not an attempt to recreate anything in nature, but to apply explicit design principles in a very particular environmental context. In an interview Fiona described her approach as 'making a painting ... I think about mass and void, texture, pulling light out, bringing the eye in and using broad foliaged textures closer and finer textures further away, to increase the depth of an area'.[51] So coastal indigenous plants have been manipulated, pruned and even topiaried, with the local moonahs trimmed so that their tortured, twisted trunks are exposed. They hang over stands of waving spear grass which create a sense of movement and fluidity with an air of extreme naturalness.

There was, however, no serious gardening to be done in inner-city Fitzroy, and I seemed to be working six long days a week and worrying about it all on the seventh. When trying to stop my mind whizzing around before going to sleep I used to imagine choosing different colours to repaint the walls in whatever house I was living in. Thinking about garden plans and the feelings that a new garden could evoke became even more therapeutic. I began to fantasise on a regular basis about a new garden that might make me feel at home on this continent, or in this south-eastern bit of it at least.

Chapter 4
Driving across the continent

Towards the end of 2007, now as settled in Melbourne as I had ever been, I found myself between jobs and in need of a temporary change of scenery and a long lie-down. I headed to the French Pyrénées where my mother still lived, on her own, in a tiny village from which her terrace looked away to the south and the eye-catching Pic du Midi d'Ossau, a mountain peak that is often described as iconic or emblematic of the Pyrénées. If you follow the annual Tour de France you will have seen the peleton strung out up one or other of its foothills, since every year a stage of the tour starts in Pau and ends somewhere up in those mountains. It is easy to love this marvellous country, where cows and sheep wear bells round their necks as they roam freely about the high pastures in summer. The local vultures may not be as big as the Australian wedge-tailed eagle, but then they know how to pick up the bones of dead cows and drop them from a great height in order to smash out the marrow. I spent a month with my mother, and then a couple of weeks in England, staying in London with a much-loved friend from my Murdoch University days. We had been bonded together since our arrival there in the mid-70s as 'foreigners' from opposite sides of the globe, both attempting to garden in the Fremantle sand (she was growing coriander while I wrestled with roses). She was a Parsee from Bombay (as she would still call it) who taught me to make proper biriyani, while her husband hosted a Reading Lenin reading group, where we all seemed to sit on the floor smoking 'roll-your-owns'. Yes, really.

My daughter was also in London, originally having a sort of delayed 'gap' year, but she had just been offered an irresistible work opportunity and was determined to stay. Her father had recently moved from Sydney to London, and was happy as a clam at the Greenwich Maritime Museum. Another dear friend, one of my first ever students at Murdoch, now lived in Oxford, and her husband had just been diagnosed with an inoperable brain tumour.

Sitting at Heathrow airport in mid-November, a glass of Qantas Club wine in my hand, waiting for my late-evening return flight to board, I realised I was suddenly and unexpectedly close to tears. There are a lot of weeping people in international airports, but in an attempt to get this under control I found a notebook in my bag, and jotted down what came into my head. This tiny notebook reappeared recently when I was moving house yet again. I had written the words 'At bottom of an emotional roller coaster' at the top of the page, and among the dot points below I had noted 'Don't feel I am going "home"'. Another dot point commented on the fact that every time I left my 90-year-old mother I wondered if I would see her again – despite the fact that she was sure her indestructible heart was going to keep her alive long after she was ready to move on. I can hear myself saying 'What am I doing getting on this plane to Australia?' I also noted that I had emailed my son in Perth to get him to ring me on my arrival back in Fitzroy, which was pretty uncharacteristic of me. But he was at least one good reason for getting on the plane.

This was not the first time I had experienced this sudden sense of disconnection from Australia, or doubts about my place here. Nor did the passing of time seem to mitigate the experience when it re-occurred (rarely, I hasten to add); it even seemed that after thirty years the distress was more acute, not less. Perhaps this is what James Wood was pointing to when he described how long it can take for the full appreciation of what has been lost to make itself felt. In my airport notes I identify other possible triggers that related to the season: 'smell and feel of autumn hitting emotional chords', 'trees turning, sycamore leaves thick underfoot', 'damp air, early evening darkness'. I find that I also made an earlier note while staying with my mother, after a Swedish childhood friend came to visit us, which led to late-night discussions about the meaning of life. It says: 'I found myself talking about buying some land on which to start a garden in Victoria. This idea has taken hold ...'

I have never kept a diary so I was surprised to unearth these notes. What I remember about sitting in the airport was the feeling that I had become unmoored by spending longer than I normally would in Europe, and in that time I had seen many people who are particularly important to me. But it is good to know the garden idea wasn't just a flash in the pan. Whether it was a project that would alleviate these symptoms and make me more confident about where I belonged was another question altogether.

I am not sure whether I was trying to evade these feelings or confront them with action, but on my return to Melbourne I distracted myself with preparations for another drive across the continent. My son had just completed his degree at the University of Western Australia, and was returning to look for work in Melbourne. My new job was not starting until the new year, so I had offered to fly over, hire a really big campervan and drive him back, along with his possessions (i.e. a bicycle, two Ikea chairs and some books) in time for Christmas. The deal was that I would drive (since he couldn't) and he would cook (since he most definitely can). We would take a week to allow for some scenic detours.

Driving sideways across the continent does not challenge one's sense of 'Australia' as much as driving from bottom to top, in my view. Plants and climate share latitude more much than longitude. The first time I flew to Sydney from Melbourne I felt I had flown from London on the Thames to Nice on the Mediterranean. Everything seemed different – the light, the humidity, the trees. Similarly, walking in the Daintree many years later I realised my hard-won Victorian forest knowledge was totally useless.

This would be my third drive across the continent. The first time I drove across from Fremantle in 1978, to meet my parents after my father suggested they would like to come and visit me in Australia. What this actually meant was that he planned to go direct to Tasmania in order to do some serious fly fishing. The fact that this was 4000 kilometres from where I was living did not seem relevant. I decided to drive across the Nullarbor and collect them (and do a little fishing myself). As someone who had only been in Australia for a couple of years, I gazed excitedly out of the panel van window, looking for something to notice. On the first day the most memorable things I passed were the extraordinary trunks of the salmon and gimlet gums on the road to Kalgoorlie, especially in the evening light, 'burnished like the flanks of a racehorse' in Seddon's memorable words.[52] Then there was the mountain containing 4 million tonnes of gold mine tailings that seemed to dominate the town of Norseman. For the next two days on the Eyre Highway the major excitement was a dead kangaroo about every hundred metres, the occasional wedge-tailed eagle, and thousands of crows. And the section of the highway marked out for light plane landings on the old 90 Mile Straight. It is now advertised as 'Australia's Longest Straight Road 145.6 kms' and was promoted in a recent glossy travel publication which features a story on 'the world's least interesting roads'.[53]

It is quite a surprise after all this when the highway suddenly drops down from the escarpment as it approaches Eucla on the South Australian border. If you stop and walk across the waves of encroaching pale sand dunes, past the old telegraph station now almost completely hidden as the sand piles up over it, you reach the Great Southern Ocean. Here you are likely to find yourself quite alone, looking out to Antarctica from the most beautiful white beach, beside the ghost of a long sea-worn jetty. From there the excitement is more regular as the road comes close to the Great Australian Bight, and then places like Streaky Bay.

I drove back to Fremantle from Melbourne with my parents a couple of weeks later, my mother sitting sideways on the mattress in the back of the panel van and knitting. We spent the night again in Eucla, staying in the luxury of the BP Motel, and I walked them over the sand dunes to the sea. It is a magical spot, and my mother, an inveterate beachcomber, understood this and picked up a small white shell from the white sand to take home with her.

The vocabulary used to describe Australian landscapes is often desolate: 'outback', 'bush', 'scrub', 'monotonous'. Some of them are of course lush and tropical. I don't think it is realistic to try to imaginatively possess the whole continent. It is so big I am unlikely to ever see most of it. I am still trying to digest my first visit to Kakadu last year, towards the end of the dry. We drove for hours through miles of flat, scrubby terrain which at that time of the year doesn't look so different to the flat, brown swathes of scrubby terrain that can be found in other parts of Australia. Then suddenly, without physical warning, you find yourself at the entrance to a narrow gorge, and after a short climb you are gazing out over a series of infinity pools to a distant view that takes your breath away. But it is a long way between spots where you feel inclined to stop and gaze or walk.

Both writers and painters have suggested that European settlers have often looked for landscapes or 'scenery' that simply don't exist in Australia. Fred Williams is best known for his later landscapes in which there are no 'focal points', but rather seamless continuity. Australians flocked to see the major retrospective of his work in Canberra in 2011 which claimed that he had 'revolutionised' the way we see and think about the Australian landscape. The exhibition title, *Infinite Horizons*, speaks to writers like Jill Ker Conway and so many others who have lived in the outback, for whom the vast horizon is what defines their sense of country. There are not many infinite horizons in England. But the challenge to the way we see here is not confined to outback vistas. George Seddon found that his move to the west coast of the continent forced him to stop looking for the Victorian landscapes of his childhood. 'Much of the interest of the landscape around Perth comes from very small things rather than from "scenery" as conventionally understood, and this change in the scale of attention is also one of the moves of science.' He learned to look for small things rather than gazing into the distance, and he only came from the other side of the country. You certainly have to learn to see if you come from Europe.

The first time I drove across the Nullarbor I had been looking for scenery and gazing into the distance. By my third crossing, this time travelling more slowly, it felt different. I did not, however, feel at home. The campervan enclosed us, carrying our shelter and food along with us, like a protective carapace. Tim Winton wrote that 'standing alone on the Nullarbor or out on a saltpan the size of a small country, you feel a twinge of terror, even in daylight, because the sky seems to go on forever'. This is the same kind of endless vista that Jill Ker Conway describes as 'akin to a religious experience', bringing real peace. There is no correct reaction to such a setting, but only those shaped by our individual histories and the way others have imaginatively apprehended the landscape, and shared that apprehension with us in some cultural form. Both Tim Winton and Jill Ker Conway feel that the Australian landscape 'imprints itself upon the body', but for the novelist, he finds that 'the mind constantly struggles to catch up and make sense of it'. He thinks that this is why, 'despite the postmodern and nearly post-physical age we live and work in, Australian writers and painters continue to obsess about landscape ... We are in a place where the material facts of life must still be contended with. There is more of it than us'.[54]

It is hard to argue with the last point when you drive across the continent or up and down it. Many years ago, when my children were very young, we drove from Melbourne to Noosa, to stay with my sister-in-law, who had moved to Perigian Beach. It is a long way. Like so many others we spent the night at Coonabarabran, in a motel with a pool from which we could collect a Chinese take away that just made it into the category of acceptable (which with young children is not a high bar). Our shared memory of this long drive centres around the enthusiasm expressed by the children's father for telescopes and the desirability of stopping to visit them, since we drove through Parkes, of course, home of the radio telescope that stars in Rob Sitch's 2000 film *The Dish*. It causes collective eye-rolling among the rest of us to this day.

On long holiday drives across France and Spain as children, my brothers and I regularly played a game which involved competitive spotting of all the letters of the alphabet, in alphabetical order, from car number plates. The relatively densely populated nature of the landscapes we drove through made this an entirely diverting game. It is not, however, a game that can be played driving to Queensland on the Newell Highway. You might never get beyond F or G. However, we were taught a new car travel game by the new brother in-law which was better suited to drives around the hinterland of Perigian Beach – a game which we still play today. It involves scanning the surrounding countryside to spot a white horse. The person who is first to shout 'white horse' is awarded a point, after argumentation about whether it really had been there, and whether it had been 'white' enough to count. It is an extremely good car game which can be played in almost any part of rural Australia.

All the way up the Newell Highway I watched both the agricultural landscape and the natural landscape slip past, wondering what crops or vegetation I was seeing. I wanted everyone with major roadside frontage to put a sign up saying what was growing there. Years later a newspaper review alerted me to the publication of the book that I had needed, and which I now keep in my glovebox: *A Traveller's Flora: A guide to familiar plants, along roadsides, in fields and forgotten places.*[55] It identifies common roadside plants, crop plants, native plants and even weeds. The author tells us that the book evolved from 'many happy holiday trips along the coast and inland with my wife, Ros, our son, Robin, his cousin Bodin, extended family and friends'. He got a small grant from the Australian Academy of Science since his aim was to encourage wider interest in botany. But in our ignorance we could at least play 'white horse' all the way back to Melbourne.

***

In 2009 my third trip across the continent began with a visit to the offices of Britz in Perth's northern suburb to collect our campervan. We headed south first, to go to the Valley of the Giants Tree Top Walk in Denmark, before setting up 'camp' on the beach near Albany. After the second night, at a perfect campsite in Cape Le Grand and a memorable walk over heathland to the beach, we headed north to Norseman where I needed to see if the tailings mountain was as impressive as I remembered it. Perhaps what had really left its mark was not so much the size of the pile, but the amount of gold that was still in it. Suffice to say, we stopped to read the sign, buy ice creams and fill the tank with diesel, but for no longer.

We steamed – driving a large diesel van somehow suggests steaming – out of Norseman heading east in the early evening, slowing for a brief unsealed patch of red dust where an emu decided to walk slowly across in front of us, with three chicks marching behind. We were listening to Paul Kelly singing 'How to make gravy' and 'Bradman' and I experienced a moment of intense happiness about where I was. At Eucla, two nights later, we parked and walked down across the rolling hills of sand to the beach where thirty years earlier my mother had collected her small shell as we drove the other way. She had given this shell to me before I left her in the Pyrénées, suggesting that we might put it back. So I had flown over to Perth with it in my bag, and now my son returned it to the beach by the jetty, and then collected a new one for us to take home. We were both strangely taken with this small ceremony.

From Eucla we pressed on to Ceduna, enjoying the sight of mallees and shrubs in Yatala National Park after so long without notable vegetation. Then suddenly we were back in wheat country, with giant silos every thirty to forty kilometres, bulging with recently harvested grain. All the way up to Port Augusta it was wheat, scrub, mallee, wheat again in a relentless cycle. It was a relief to see Iron Knob rising up on the horizon. It reminded me of my surprised amusement

when I learned how Lang Hancock 'discovered' the world's largest iron ore deposit in the Pilbara. 'Discover' is a thoroughly inflated verb for this achievement, since the ore was sitting on the ground and he just had to be flying over it and look out of the window at the right time. It is a salutary reminder that so much Australian wealth has been easily won.

After a night near Wilpena in the Flinders Ranges, and a shared sense of mild disappointment in Wilpena Pound, compounded by the heat perhaps, we headed back out to the south, through Hawker to Peterborough to join the Sturt Highway. Here we were travelling close to the Goyder line, drawn by the South Australian Surveyor General in 1865 – the line demarcating areas suitable for farming from those where there would not be enough rainfall. As ill-luck would have it ample rains fell that year, and farmers ignored his report and moved north to settle and plant crops. The tragic idea that rain follows the plough took hold, encouraging more settlement north of the line. The rain did not last long, and as you drive through this grim landscape you can see the ruined old farmhouses, abandoned so soon, harsh evidence of Goyder's wisdom. As if to ram this history home we found ourselves in a dust storm with high winds, threatening clouds, strange orange light, low visibility, creating a general air of desolation as backdrop to the ruins near Carrieton and Orroroo.

There is a photograph of a long-abandoned stone cottage near the town of Burra that is just like hundreds of others through the mid-north of South Australia, except that this one was used on the cover of Midnight Oil's 1987 album *Diesel and Dust*. The startling and beautiful picture of the decaying building, surrounded by bone-dry paddocks, has been used to promote tourism in the region and The Australian Children's Choir, scattered around those paddocks, sang to make us feel warm about Qantas. It is clearly a powerful image of Australia, a piece of very sunburnt country surrounded by sweeping plains. But it is not clear that anyone wants to tell the sad story behind it.

It was a relief to arrive in the 'historic' mining town of Burra and set up camp by the river in the centre of town. The next morning we decided to skip Broken Hill and head towards Renmark. There is more depressing dry brown countryside that looks like it has been overstocked until we get back into wheat country, and then arrive on the Murray River at Morgan, where suddenly we are surrounded by the intense green of irrigated citrus groves. Oranges are falling off the trees as we drive along the south bank of the Murray, but there are also great swampy stretches of land and water, inhabited by sad dead trees. Around Mildura the abandoned vineyards signal a warning about the difficulties the region faces. But we find a campsite on the New South Wales side of the river with a million-dollar aspect, and smooth lawn sloping from our allocated camping spot down to the mighty Murray. It is my first experience of the Murray. There is a warm breeze, those famous river red gums, and pelicans. I have written PERFECT in capital letters in the notes I kept about how many kilometres we did each day and where we spent each night. We walked over the bridge into Mildura, a town that wilfully turns its back on the river, prepared to splash out in a big way, but have to make do with eating in a venue that sits on top of Stefano de Pieri's eponymous restaurant. We had failed to book in advance.

The campervan has to be returned the next day to its home in Braybrook, out in the western suburbs of Melbourne, so there is a lot of driving to do. We steamed down the Calder Highway, noticing only the unrelenting fields of wheat and the grain transport trucks hauling the harvest, while each town marked on the map turned out to be only a huge silo, and an opportunity to buy diesel and a sandwich if we were lucky.

By the time we pulled into my narrow home street in Fitzroy, after more than 4000 kilometres of road, I was no longer wondering what I was doing in Australia. I had a new job which I thought I could do well, and which would take me into regional Victoria more often. Within a year I started to look for a place in the country.

Chapter 5
Living in the country and learning about the wildlife

I did not want a holiday home near the beach, nor a piece of native bush. I wanted 'a place in the country' in the way a French or English woman might use the phrase. This means somewhere rural and preferably pretty, where the land is primarily used for agriculture of some kind, and where you might also feel yourself close to nature; in a landscape still shaped by its past and home to indigenous flora and fauna. I needed enough land to have a large garden, but had no intention of farming anything myself. However, I was not looking for an escape from city pressures, nor did I imagine myself finally sitting down to read Marcel Proust's *In Search of Lost Time*. I was looking for something to *do*, and a place where I could gradually spend more and more of my time. I don't like it when friends joke about my endless need for new projects as this suggests that I have no deep master plan for my life, or that I have no still centre. It makes me sound as though I am just looking for things to keep me busy. But it is also true that I looked forward not just to having a glorious country garden but to making this glorious country garden. And I should admit that when I realised I was going to need a ride-on mower I was as happy as a child with their first tricycle. I am the practical kind of person who really loves going to Bunnings, even as I bemoan the loss of neighbourhood ironmongers, and the miserable quality of the chrome on anything made in China.

My search terms defined a 150-kilometre arc around Melbourne from the north to the south west coast, from Kyneton round to Lorne. Anywhere to the east felt too unfamiliar, while the Yarra Valley and the Mornington Peninsula were out of my financial league. When I later read Robert Kenny's memoir and his description of what he wanted from his home in the country I understood him completely. Like him, I had no interest in living in 'pristine nature', nor in a forest. As he put it:

> I wanted to live in farming country ... But somehow too I wanted to get close, not to an imagined nature, but to life. To the wildlife yes, but also to the productivity of the human engagement with the land. What I wanted to do there beside work was to garden. Primarily I wanted to create a garden, perhaps in some ways a productive one, but primarily as a space to be in, to enjoy. Yes, a couple of acres, I thought.[56]

I, too, fondly imagined finding a couple of acres. But here we both ran into the scale problem in Australia. Planning provisions in Victoria mean that you are highly unlikely to find a couple of acres except on the edge of a small town, and I did not want to be on the edge of a town. Where land is zoned for farming, which is the kind we both wanted, it may not be subdivided in lots less than 40 hectares. That is 100 acres. Kenny ended up having to buy 70 acres.

I went to look at a very large, flat paddock near Woodend with a fine view to Hanging Rock; a very charming 'cottage' on the Campaspe which I was already wise enough to know would go way over the reserve at auction; and a couple of potato paddocks in Murroon which looked across the narrow road to a small vineyard, making me think for a brief moment it would do – despite its manifest unsuitability in every other respect. Nearly everything I saw required an implausible amount of imaginative investment or a huge bank balance.

On one occasion I drove down past Geelong towards the Otways to look at a block of land just south-east of Deans Marsh. I had already widened my realestate.com.au search terms to allow much larger properties into my field of vision. This one was 31 acres, situated in an out-of-the-way little pocket of unsealed roads that run along the top of one low ridge and back along the next one. If you didn't do the return loop you could exit on a rarely used – and unevenly maintained – back road, heading south-east to Aireys Inlet through a major pine plantation and then through bushland in the Great Otway National Park. This small, hidden-away locality was a very nice surprise, with its rolling hills, a wooded narrow valley running between the two ridges, sudden spectacular long views away to the north, and small paddocks along the roadside. I did not have to exercise my imagination too hard to envisage living there, and I knew that back road out to Aireys Inlet from beach holidays with the children when they were young. I also knew the pine plantation was an excellent source of pine mushrooms.

However, the block of land, with no house on it, somehow intimidated me. Leaning over the gate, with its handsome old carved sign saying 'Blackwood', I could see Angus cattle through the acacias and gum trees. I felt out of my depth. I just wanted to have a garden, for heaven's sake.

Perhaps two years after that failure of nerve another property came up for sale, on the opposite ridge, with a mere 28 acres. This time there was a house of indeterminate age but with good bones, and a large garden sloping down behind the house towards a paddock. This left the back of the house jutting out over the ground in a rather unsatisfactory way. True, the deck along the back offered spectacular views to the north, and a pair of wedge-tailed eagles could be seen, circling in the warm updrafts. But from the rear, there was none of that desirable 'settling' into the landscape that is admired in the best of *Grand Designs*. As in so much of rural Australia, the building looked plonked down from somewhere else, which I discovered was because it had indeed been plonked down from somewhere else. It was an Edwardian timber house, uprooted twenty years earlier from

its original setting in the Melbourne suburb of Caulfield and transported to this block of land in three pieces. With it came an acorn, collected from under one of the biggest oak trees in Darling Gardens, Clifton Hill. The handsome original period verandah had been removed (I found it afterwards under the house), and a bull-nosed, Victorian-era version had been added to three sides of the house. The result was not very pretty, but certainly functional. The owner was known for hanging her sheets along the balustrades to dry.

I later discovered that many houses in the region had been transported from Melbourne. No wonder it is hard to read the landscape in these rural neighbourhoods. The eventual purchaser of 'Blackwood' had, in the meantime, bought an excellent little 1960s weatherboard house in Torquay that was about to be demolished, paying $6000 plus a site cleaning fee. He then paid a great deal more than that to have it transported on to his block, where it sat perfectly in the landscape, in what I came to think of as the best setting for miles around. I experienced envy, or at least the opposite of buyer's remorse, when I ended up sitting in his kitchen discussing the state of our paddocks, fences or the price of hay, looking out through his stand of fine old gum trees.

My 'Edwardian' house had been owned by Noelle, a nursery woman, and out of the bare paddock where the house was deposited she had created a large garden full of interesting plants and trees, all of which were 'exotic', and all of which were exotically distributed. There was also a substantial vegetable garden, though it is better understood as several areas for growing fruit and vegetables than what I would really call a garden. The large asparagus bed, for example, was set slightly at an angle in some grass just to the back of the house, and there were three long rows of worked-over soil (not really 'beds' as I would understand the term) through which she rotated large crops of onions, tomatoes and brassicas. In another part of the garden were three cherry trees professionally trained in what I learn is called the Tatura trellis system, an innovation developed by the Victorian Department of Agriculture and now used around the world. Further down the slope were three plum trees and a prune d'Agen, then six apple trees perfectly pruned for fruiting and picking over a long season, a quince and a mulberry. Yet further down the garden was a curved row of blackcurrant bushes, in danger of being strangled by a spreading mass of wachendorfias, which are as crazed as they sound. One tiny plant liberated by Noelle from the Geelong Botanic Gardens had turned into an indestructible 30-metre strip of dense foliage marking the end of the garden.

Everywhere else in the garden were randomly drawn beds, edged with dead branches in rustic style, filled with a fine variety of plants familiar to a Kentish maid like me. There were salvias, hydrangeas, Japanese anemones, hellebores, spirea, buddleias, viburnum, philadelphus, but also others I had never met before. Large swathes of daffodils had naturalised under the great Darling Garden oak tree on the front lawn as well as across the bottom of the garden as it transitioned into paddock.

Dotted around the garden, according to a logic that I could never discern was one (or sometimes two) of just about every exotic tree you might care to have – although perhaps not in the Otways. There was a crabapple, magnolia grandiflora, plane tree, sycamore, ash (*Fraxinus*), catalpa, scarlet oak and pin oak as well as the English oak from the Clifton Hill acorn, Japanese maple, ornamental weeping cherry and a liquidamber, among others. This was a plantswoman's garden. It was in no sense a blank sheet waiting for my creative imprint.

The maker of this garden left me an A3-sized map with key plants noted on it, just in case I should miss anything. It would, it turned out, have been more helpful to inherit a map of the miles of poly pipes running underground that kept all this watered – pipes that I inevitably stabbed with my fork or cut in half with my spade as I gradually began reshaping the layout. The gardened part of the property overwhelmed me for quite a while, if I am honest. It took me too long to realise that I should remove almost everything except the fruit trees and start again, with some serious hard landscaping and terracing.

There was more to my property than the garden, however. The area I had settled into was zoned for farming, but it was unsuited to any kind of farming that made money. It is characterised by rolling hills and small, not very fertile, sloping paddocks. In the immediate area the only serious form of farming seemed to be agro-forestry and viticulture. A small vineyard nearby made a very good pinot. I'd offered a wine-loving friend one of my sloping north-facing paddocks if he would plant vines, subject to a proper soil test, but I had taken so long to find a place he had given up on me and bought on the other side of Port Phillip Bay. It would have been a perfect arrangement.

So instead of vines, I was left with a famously bad-tempered and uncontrollable cow (an Angus/Limousin cross) who survived because she was always fat and glossy and could pop out a calf without drama. She was kept company by a small group of famously even-tempered Belted Galloways belonging to the neighbours. I kept on with the arrangement so that the grass would be eaten down, and to have calves, and then home-killed beef. Belted Galloways are not only well mannered and delicious but also a picturesque addition to the landscape.

The front boundary of the property was a strip of remnant bush. I know this because a little way back along the very pretty, tree-lined unsealed road was a sign, designating this stretch as remnant bush, and admonishing over-zealous council workers NOT TO SPRAY. I did not know – yet – what the large eucalypts and acacias were, let alone the smaller understorey shrubs. I did know that they ran across the garden on its south side and so were unlikely to present a direct fire risk. A nicely treed gully ran through the bottom of the property on the northern edge – with a small flow of water in winter, and a series of well-defined muddy paths in and out that I later realised were

kept open by a small mob of kangaroos. The area was well separated from the house by a couple of grass paddocks, so this bit of bush also presented no direct fire risk. All in all, around the property there was sufficient habitat for a variety of native birds and animals.

Birds

When I inspected the house, I had noticed that Noelle kept a birdbath on the rear deck, a spot from which you felt you could see all the way to Ballarat – or Winchelsea at least. This seemed an unlikely place for such a thing, but she insisted birds came if she sat still. So I bought a terracotta birdbath at Bunnings, and after reading a bit about how birds might use it, placed it at the far end of the deck (which ran the width of the house), near a flourishing tall viburnum bush in which small birds could hide while they summoned up the courage to bathe. The first visitors to the house needed no encouragement, however. A family of king parrots walked up and down the balustrade on a regular basis and I was told they expected pine-nut offerings – which I was not going to continue. A thrush took up residence in some old shelving left on the front deck, and I could see that swifts regularly nested up under the bullnose verandah on the western side, leaving large deposits on the decking underneath. I knew a parrot or a

swift when I saw one, but the thrush was a bird I had to look up. Unlike most Australian birds, the grey shrike-thrush sings in a very delightful way. The fact that it seemed unfussed by human activity so near the nest that it was busy constructing in the shelves added to its charm.

Walking or driving along my road, there was always the chance of crimson rosellas zooming along in front like small guided missiles. Other birds I might never have noticed without help. My local builder, who might almost qualify as a twitcher, would occasionally arrive later than usual, perhaps because he had stopped to confirm a sighting of whistling ducks on his way over; or would pause in his work to say things like 'there's that azure kingfisher'. I would ask where. He would tell me to listen. I would listen and pretend I could hear the sound, and with luck he would point to a fence post or overhanging branch and say 'Over there'. I needed lessons in how to spot them because they are so small and so fast in the air. I did eventually learn to see them as somehow their little flashes of white do stand out, but I did not learn to notice their song.

I kept a pair of binoculars by the back door and a notebook for birds that I spotted, as I am a slightly competitive person when it comes to lists and games. More easily spotted was a trail of small blue objects leading into an impenetrable little bit of native vegetation behind my concrete water tank. Following the trail I found what must be a bower, with its carpet of blue baler twine, blue straws, blue biro parts, the odd blue bottle top and some random twigs. I am excited by this discovery, and even more so by the sight of the very handsome, glossy blue-black satin bowerbird I later notice hopping around near the water tank.

A year later I know better. Any sign of a bower being built and I am out there demolishing it, removing the blue booty, and watching out for any in the nearby roadside vegetation. The scales fell from my eyes when I noticed that something had been attacking my carefully nurtured carrots. Their tops were torn off, and there were multiple stab wounds to any part of the carrot that was close to the surface. These were not inflicted by the usual suspects, namely rabbits and kangaroos. I asked my neighbours what else I should be worried about, and learned that I should suspect bowerbirds. My neighbours were admittedly pleased that the bowerbirds were all with me as they tend to move en masse from one house to another at different times. 'Are they with you?' we would ask each other, hopefully, as special crops ripened.

I never caught them at work on my carrots, but I did see them sometime later at work in a rather disfigured hawthorn shrub that had been planted on the eastern fence-line of the garden, so close to the fence that the cattle chewed on any part they could reach. I kept it for several years because in autumn it produced the most impressive crop of yellow berries, the size of small apricots. The fruit of the hawthorn is well known for attracting birds, but on this day there was a very high level of activity, with birds taking it in turn to fly into the bush at full speed, tear off a fruit, and fly out again. Not caring about the fate of the berries, I got my binoculars to watch. They were substantial olive-green birds with very muscular beaks, flying like fighter planes in and out, with no fluttering or hesitation. It was a squadron of female and immature male bowerbirds.

It turned out that they were interested in much more than carrots and yellow berries, having the focus and beak power to destroy any crop they fancied. I noticed them in the small feijoa I had inherited, holding a fruit with one foot while pecking away at it (but felt no need to intervene as I don't understand why anyone eats feijoas). If you are lucky the wrecking squad finds better things to eat on your neighbour's property. But what I now understand is that we have in fact been accidentally encouraging them, since it is the planting of exotic trees and shrubs that carry beautiful berries like cotoneaster and holly, as well as hawthorn, which has made these invasions worse. In winter, without these new menu options, bowerbirds would have had to turn to leaves to keep them going, but we were offering them something much more delicious. Satin bowerbirds not only swarm into the berry-filled winter gardens of Canberra, but then proceed to spread those exotic plants through the bush.[57]

It is not surprising that the Australian countryside is covered in tree-netting as carefully grown fruit begins to ripen. The netting is not pretty, though. I planted a rather pretentious espaliered pear walk because a neighbour gave me a bargain on six trees that he had been espaliering in pots for several years, and a cooked pear is one of my favourite things. Once the trees were mature enough to produce a good number of pears, I netted each one with its own little white bag, closed with a drawstring at the top. Over the months as they ripened every single un-netted pear was eaten, but I felt smug about my netting bags which looked so much nicer than the full body treatment. In late March, after a few days in town, I returned and did my usual tour of the garden. On the ground was every single pear bag,

each with a hole torn in it. How the bags/pears were removed from the tree I cannot say, but they were now empty. Nothing left. Nada.

A few days later new neighbours who spent half the week in town and half the week next door emailed me to ask if I had seen anyone on their property because their whole netted apple and pear crop, which was almost commercial in size, had been stripped. Apparently the thief had also cleaned up all the apples on the ground underneath the industrial netting. For a brief period I let myself think that someone might have done this. But then it dawned on me that my neighbours were even more naive than I was about country life, and that we had both almost certainly suffered from a major attack by the bowerbird squadron. They cleaned up the fallen apples not to hide their traces but to maximise their calories.

Australian birds do take some getting used to. Much has been written about how early European visitors and settlers found them certainly colourful, but also noisy – and not in a good way. To European ears Australian birds did not sing.[58] As a visiting naturalist remarked in 1854 there are 'several chirpers, a few Whistlers many screamers, Screechers, & yelpers, but no songsters among the birds here'.[59] And this reaction hasn't changed much since. 'The great bowerbird's hissing is described in a 2001 guide as a cross between tearing paper and violent vomiting.'[60] Every baby who has been read Alison Lester's *Roar* knows that the sulphur-crested cockatoo, when asked 'What do you say?', replies 'Squawk, squawk, squawk'. I did not grow up here reading children's story books in which kookaburras battle with snakes, knowing only the great Rikki Tikki Tavi, the heroic snake-defying mongoose from Rudyard Kipling's imperial *Jungle Tales*. Despite lacking grounds for admiring this unusual bird, it is impossible not to feel cheered by its crazed song. Don Watson's evocation of evenings in the country when 'the cockatoos have quietened, the last of the little birds have settled somewhere and that cathedral silence has fallen' tells me how the kookaburra works in the Victorian imagination. Silence does fall. But then 'a kookaburra laughs, then another, then another, and the trees seem to be shaking with the mad sound. If nothing else will pin you to your native land, this will.'[61]

Many Australian birds make me and probably most of us laugh, while I can't think of an English bird that is particularly funny. But the most thrilling bird I have seen in the country was a powerful owl which only rarely called, and which I first saw when the dam pump came on in the middle of a moonlit night, signalling a leak somewhere. I got up, got the torch and headed outside under the house to turn it off, knowing it would otherwise keep me awake. I opened the back door, and as I did so a very large grey bird launched itself effortlessly from the top of my enclosed vegetable garden and glided low over the rear terrace as I desperately tried to focus my torch on it. I knew a powerful owl hunted nearby, as it left evidence of its presence in the form of clinically eviscerated rabbit remains on my lawn.

The bird that I feel most fond of is the tawny frogmouth, for its wild eyebrows, crazed expression, genius camouflage against the branches of a melaleuca, and lack of interest in my crops. I found the colours of most other Australian birds dazzling after the thrushes, sparrows and blackbirds of my childhood. An intimidating woman from a nearby council housing estate, who came to help my mother in the house when we were little, had a caged yellow budgerigar, which she let fly around her tiny sitting room from time to time. I had no idea where budgerigars lived and they didn't seem real. I confess that Mrs Wood didn't seem real either.

Just as I began to take a closer interest in Australian birds, out of necessity as well as opportunity, biologist Tim Low's book, *Where Song Began: Australia's Birds and How They Changed theWorld*, was published. Not only does he explain why our birds screech a lot, but in doing so he explains even more about this continent's unique trees. It is a gripping account of the way our flora and bird life evolved together in this harsh dry environment, and since Low is one of those scientists who knows how to engage his audience, it should most definitely be on the reading list for new citizens – if perhaps in a shorter version.

The trees of my childhood, and the northern hemisphere generally, rely on the wind to carry pollen between trees. The resulting fruit is dispersed in ingenious ways, with the heavy sycamore seed requiring a long wing to help it spiral through the air like a helicopter, while the elm's fruit is surrounded by a dry round wing which helps it to fly far and wide on the wind. Trees relying on the wind do not need flowers to attract birds and insects for pollination, but the horse chestnut is an obvious exception in the English countryside, with its large, spectacular, insect-attracting flowers. It then relies on animals to carry off the very large seeds to winter storage places where some will germinate.

What is so remarkable (to us from the north) is that nearly all Australian plants are pollinated by birds. I had heard the mountain ash to be found around Melbourne (*Eucalyptus regnans*) described as 'the world's tallest flowering plant', but I had not understood what kind of competition this really was since surely it was more important to be the world's tallest tree. And I was initially more interested in its need to burn. But for there to be seeds to germinate in a terrible fire, there has to be pollination. When a very large lemon-scented gum in the garden next to my small Fitzroy house flowered it would be invaded during the daytime by flocks of rosellas and by hordes of fruit bats in the evening. Until I read Low I did not understand the significance of this, and how whole forests are dominated by large nectar-feeding birds, without which pollination would not occur. Nor had I wondered how these large birds could survive on nectar.

Other countries have tiny nectar feeders like hummingbirds, but ours are colossal by comparison. Wattlebirds, Low tells us, were hunted by settlers almost to extinction, requiring a bag limit of fifteen birds a day until the 1960s when catching them was finally banned. But as late as 1991 Low was told by a poacher about the pleasures of wattlebird stew, with the yellow fat congealing on top to be skimmed off as butter. Just think, Low writes, 'nectar in flowers ending up as butter on the homestead table. Red wattlebirds were sold in Sydney's poultry shops in large numbers. They were pronounced the best eating bird in the bush'.[62]

Many Australian birds are loud and aggressive because it is worth their while scaring other birds away from a flower source. 'A fruit, seed or insect is gone after it is eaten, but flowers supply nectar hour after hour, often day after day. More than other foods, flowers reward aggression.'[63] Anyone who is interested in gardening with native plants knows that the most tempting flowering shrubs come from the south-west of Western Australia (which makes many of them unhappy in the heavy clay soils to be found all over Victoria). The banksias of that region are particularly reliable sources of nectar, and the western wattlebird is vigilant in controlling its sugar supply. Nineteenth-century English ornithologist John Gould described it as 'very pugnacious, attacking every bird, both large and small, that approaches its domicile'.[64]

I have always cheered on the yellow wattlebirds in Fitzroy and Northcote as they scare off the invasive and ubiquitous Indian mynah birds ('flying rats' or the 'cane toads of the sky'), but now I understood why they are so raucous and so belligerent. If you could choose between listening to a nightingale and a wattlebird there would surely be no contest. But I no longer hear the loud, harsh noises made by so many Australian birds as something weird, or disconcerting. I know what they are up to, and it all makes perfect evolutionary sense. They are not doing it to annoy us. Making a sound as though you are vomiting or tearing paper is intended to be off-putting.

My bird 'studies' (dilettante in nature) were greatly enhanced by installing the Australian Birds app developed by ornithologists Michael Morcombe and David Stewart on my phone. It provides information on hundreds of Australian birds, indexed in different ways, with each page providing the clearest of drawings to help identify a bird correctly, together with a map of its distribution, and most usefully, recordings of the calls made by birds in different situations. It asks you to use the bird calls 'sparingly and briefly', and enjoins us at all times to try 'not to disturb the birds or interfere with the enjoyment of other bird observers, who may well prefer to listen out for the real calls'. This is birding etiquette at its best.

The fact that I had inherited a garden full of the plants that I was trying to wean myself off turned out to be good from the bird point of view (and the bee point of view). When the indigenous trees and shrubs were not in flower I was providing plenty of alternative nectar sources. All through summer eastern spinebills perched happily in horizontal position with their long, curved bills poked into the tall kniphofias (not the red-hot ones, but tasteful lime pokers), looking like proper honeyeaters. It was on an extremely floriferous ceanothus bush that I first saw a blue banded bee, was mesmerised by it, and spent a ridiculous amount of time trying to capture it on my phone. I had no idea such an insect existed.

Roses thrived on the clay of the Otway foothills, and it was hard to resist having a lot of them now I had so much space. One summer afternoon, leaning in to dead-head David Austin's Ambrose rose growing in one of my long perennial beds, I am startled by some rapid movement just below my arm. It is snake season so adrenalin is easily aroused. But it is just a superb fairy wren whizzing out of her nest, which sits sideways in a shrubby salvia, almost at ground level. I lift a couple of straggly shoots and bend down to look in. Eggs, definitely. I quickly step back and tell myself to avoid pruning around here for a while.

Over the next couple of weeks I accidentally disturb her more than once, and she flashes out and away into a large grevillea leaning over the concrete water tank where many birds take refuge from time to time (including spinebills when they are harassed by thuggish wattlebirds). One morning, as I take a peek to see how things are coming along, I see a young face at the nest entrance, and the fledgling it is attached to immediately flies out. Well, it flaps out, landing in the nearest plant. It then has another go – definite improvement – and reaches the nearby buddleia, where it lands on a dazzling carmine blossom. It looks more like a furry ping-pong ball than a bird, missing the distinctive perky adult wren's tail. From the buddleia it has another go at take-off – but now its father is worried. I see him perched on the top of a very tall dark canna lily stem, easily visible with his beautiful blue cap, cheeks and scarf. I subsequently learn that there is a very good chance this is not the father, with superb fairy wrens having some of the highest levels of female infidelity ever detected in birds.[65] The fledgling's mother is also hovering nearby. The baby, now over-confident, launches itself out of the perennial bed and into the nearby herb garden where it crashes, luckily toppling into a clump of chives. Now the parents are circling, perhaps more anxious because the baby is calling loudly. But this is clearly the end of the practice run, as suddenly the baby is off. And later when I check the nest, no one has come home. It seems they are now an airborne family.

Perhaps it is too easy to love Australian fairy wrens as they do not eat my vegetables or fruit, preferring insects and spiders, and they do not screech. Boring brown wrens are to be found all over England so the blue makes them much more interesting, though I think they are in fact unrelated. Nonetheless it is their shared perky tails which make them instantly recognisable. The most familiar bird to me, however, both in Melbourne and the Otways, was the blackbird, scourge of neat gardeners for its habit of scratching mulch on to pathways or lawn as it looks for a meal wriggling beneath the soil. The song of a blackbird at dawn is a sound that powerfully reminds me of springtime in England, somehow triggering a sense of happiness and the anticipation of sunshine and warmth, which, in England, counts for a lot.

Blackbird song is so familiar that I had never thought about whether it was beautiful or not. But now I want to know more about its effects on me I discover that I am not alone in my reaction. According to the British Library:

> The blackbird has been called the Beethoven among birds. The cock sings long, beautifully shaped phrases, well-defined in time and tone. The effect is mellow, flute-like and musical. Joseph Addison (1672–1719) wrote 'I value my garden more for being full of blackbirds than of cherries, and very frankly give them fruit for their songs'. [66]

It should not be surprising that early settlers in Victoria sought to introduce those birds that reminded them most intensely of 'Old England', and it is hard not to be moved by their commitment to this project. Robert Morrice, 'a settler of many years standing' sponsored the importation of a small number of desirable birds, working indefatigably to keep them alive on the passage from England:

> The precious little cargo of twelve larks, a nightingale, a goldfinch and two or three other songbirds sailed from England in October 1853. Four larks and all the other birds sickened and died during the voyage, and though eight were safely landed at Melbourne one died soon afterwards. Morrice then set free the seven tired and frightened survivors on the Barrabool Hills, near Geelong.[67]

An Acclimatisation Society was formed in 1861, and enthusiastically monitored the release of more songbirds into the Botanic Gardens in Melbourne. These included eighteen blackbirds, twenty-four thrushes, eight starlings and another six skylarks.[68] Here it gets harder to see any of this as benign, as starlings have become an agricultural pest and do not sing in exchange. The acclimatisers followed this up with the Indian mynah among others. As we know, the skylarks and nightingales died very quickly, leaving us with the starlings and mynahs, and the blackbirds. The 2020 Aussie Backyard Bird Count reported that the three most commonly seen birds in Tasmania were the sparrow, the starling and the blackbird. It was almost a relief to see that the Rainbow Lorikeet dominates almost everywhere else, which BirdLife Australia puts down to the increasing use of native flowering plants in suburban gardens.

I was initially happy to hear blackbird song in the Otways. But living part-time in the country was definitely shifting my centre of gravity as within a couple of years I was ready to wage guerrilla war on them. To my surprise I had turned them into invasive pests, as they squabble with native birds (as well as damaging commercial fruit crops and constantly fossicking in my mulch). I discovered that they are actually prohibited in Western Australia. I took my cue from the previous owner when I heard about her cunning plan to reduce their numbers. This involved finding the blackbird nest, discreetly removing the eggs, boiling them for a few minutes, and then returning them to the nest, still warm. Destroying the eggs and nest would simply encourage the birds to build another nest and lay more eggs. Putting them back, cooked, would keep the parents safely occupied for a few weeks at least, with no young ones to show for it. The tricky part was getting the mother to leave her nest long enough for me to steal the eggs. But once I saw them simmering in a saucepan I laughed aloud at this evidence of my adaptation. Better late than never. I liked the boisterous song of the shrike-thrush, the plaintive cries of gang-gang cockatoos going overhead, and the conversational cheeping from the family of king parrots noisily eating the seeds in my Japanese maples. A magpie warbling now triggers just the same feelings of recognition and affection and possibly belonging. This country business seemed to be working.

Rats, kangaroos and echidnas

Making a garden and growing fruit and vegetables is, I discovered, as likely to make you hate indigenous wildlife as love it. Most of my neighbours, despite their green politics, talked about the struggle to protect their gardens as a form of warfare, and would happily shoot an aggressive possum or bowerbirds if they stayed still long enough.

I knew nothing about bush rats until I almost broke an ankle after catching a gumboot in the entrance to what turned out to be one of several burrows in my perennial flower beds. The fact that it was a rat, albeit an Australian rat with the charming rounded ears of a mouse, initially put it in the 'eliminate' category. Perhaps I also imagined them undermining my favourite shrubs with their tunnelling. After a while I wondered if, really, they did any harm. My campaign against them became half-hearted. But in the end I tightened my line on them again after Tim Low wrote that bush rats (*Rattus fuscipes*) 'are little different from the rats (*R. rattus*) that gave Europe the plague'.[69] I was lucky never to have any resident possums, since some brushtails along the ridge were known to attack dogs as well as destroying plant life. By far the biggest threat was posed by birds, which meant covering the fruit trees in netting for months on end, rendering them hideous to look at, as well as ensnaring the odd snake.

In the end I did the obvious thing and built a large fully enclosed vegetable garden in which I could espalier new apple and plum trees and grow whatever I wanted with only aphids and caterpillars to worry about. I had watched the fiendishly clever pied currawongs learn to bounce up and down on the annual netting over the cherry trees so that they could get closer to the buds and fruit, and knew I needed something that resembled a netted fort to keep them and the bowerbirds at bay. Such an enclosure was also the single sure-fire defence against rabbit incursions, which only the periodic distribution of a new *calicivirus* seemed to control. Sometimes I would drive in the front gate to find forty or fifty rabbits trimming the front lawn. I had recently discovered that it was close by, at Barwon Park in Winchelsea, that English settler Thomas Austin had made several attempts to introduce the English rabbit, 'before his efforts were crowned with undreamed of success', as the historian of the Western District, Margaret Kiddle, so elegantly put it. Among other motives, Austin was keen to provide suitable sporting opportunities on his 30 000 acre property for the Duke of Edinburgh's visit in 1867. There is nothing much left to say about these rabbits, except that their perfectly acclimatised descendants caused predictable mayhem in my garden, not just eating grass but digging holes in the lawns to get at the roots. I did get a gun licence and at least imagined picking them off from my back deck as they hopped up the paddock in the late afternoon to feed on my labours.

The only animal that made a hole in my kitchen garden netting was a large kangaroo which tried to jump through it, not noticing it while nibbling on the salvia growing against it. After a very long dry

spell kangaroos had decided that my lawn was the best thing going for them, closely followed by rose bushes. The house was now surrounded on all sides by well-moisturised lawn because that seemed the best form of protection against the risk of a grass fire, and I had a large dam and a lot of poly pipes everywhere, so no shortage of available water – until the pump broke down, a pop-up sprinkler failed to rise out of the ground, or a leak developed, all of which happened quite often. There was no way to keep the kangaroos out of the garden, so for a while my first task of the day was raking up kangaroo poo.

There is something so ordinary and yet so extraordinary about the kangaroo that I still don't really know what I feel about them. Such large and unusual creatures remain disconcerting despite their ubiquity, and even though they are so shy my neighbours had warned me about the way they could and would attack a dog if cornered by one. One morning there was a large male standing up on my front verandah as I came round the corner. After several years I still found their proximity somehow foreign or even exotic, when of course it is I who am foreign if not exotic. When teenage joeys jumped into their mothers' pouches leaving their large haunches hanging out, they were just very funny. When much younger joeys peeped out to chew grass while their mothers were bent over doing the same, they were irresistible.

For international visitors, Australian mammals are an unusual lot. An elderly German colleague told me that he grew up learning that Australia was a backward continent full of half-finished animals: the kangaroo with two small arms and two huge legs, mammals laying eggs as though they belonged to some earlier evolutionary era, or having pouches because their young are born too soon. If I had really become Australian, would I take kangaroos for granted, and see them as the equivalent of rabbits in England or deer in North America – as prolific breeders when the environment is supportive and highly adaptable to man-made changes in their landscape, capable of becoming just a 'pest'? Or does their sheer size make their proximity startling?

I think that easily the most charming visitor to the garden was the echidna. In fact she was probably a resident rather than a visitor, though I never managed to be sure about the exact location of her home. She would appear from time to time moving slowly along a

particular route across the garden, under the house and out the other side, heading towards the paddock. The joy of your own echidna is that you can catch up to her and then stand very still until she decides it is safe to uncurl and continue digging up insects at your feet. Given the success Beatrix Potter had with Mrs Tiggywinkle, the hedgehog, I am surprised that echidnas do not feature more than wombats in Australian children's stories. Wombats (which are not be found in my part of the Otways) often appear as thoroughly destructive characters, with only their generic 'bear' shape to make them appear loveable.[70] The echidna by contrast has the most delightful snout and face, and it is hard not to laugh when you see them walking.[71]

I had long forgotten my basic introduction to the 'weirdness' of Australian mammals, when you learn about the platypus that defies all zoological categories. Having an echidna close by that was quite happy to dig round my unmoving feet renewed my interest. I was unlikely to see it lay eggs, but I could easily see that it did not walk so much as waddle, its legs designed more for digging than forward movement. There was also something profoundly reassuring about the way it simply curled up when it sensed any danger, giving it an aura of invincibility. You didn't have to feel worried or guilty about an echidna.

One day from the house I saw what looked like a molehill moving in the paddock and got out my binoculars to check in on the echidna's movements. I was surprised to see that she appeared to be being followed, slowly, by two more echidnas. I guessed this might be the mating season as I had never seen a second echidna around, so I belatedly looked for more information about them. I discovered that the fact that echidnas lay eggs is far less interesting than how they get pregnant. I cannot put it better than this:

> From mid-May to early September, male echidnas actively seek out females to mate. They form a line known as an 'echidna train', with the female leading the 'train', followed by up to ten males. A smaller, younger male is often at the rear of the line.
>
> The male suitors follow the female for long distances until the female is ready to mate. She then lies relaxed and flat on her stomach and the males that formed the 'train' dig a circular trench around her. Eventually the largest male pushes the competing rivals out of this 'mating rut'. He then digs more dirt out from the spot where the female's tail is resting, lies on his side and places his tail under hers, and they mate. [72]

I kept my binoculars trained on the paddock until my arms ached hoping to witness this spectacle and then gave up. I didn't want to get any closer for fear of interfering. From Tom Keneally's ode to the echidna I learn that what I am missing is even more interesting, as male echidnas have four penises, and use two at any one time to respond to the female's 'bifurcated genitals', keeping two in reserve for next time. It seems Keneally loves the echidna as I do: 'it gives off an air, despite its limited movement, of industry, and has the sort of waddle that in humans is the mark of elderly groundkeepers you have to charm before you're allowed to do anything.'[73]

Ants, spiders and snakes

It is amusing, in an admittedly childish way, to alert European or North American visitors to the extraordinarily venomous nature of Australian snakes and spiders. Most city dwellers are unlikely to come across a venomous snake, or to know whether they have been near one, though in Melbourne warning signs are displayed near creeks and rivers about what to do if your dog is bitten by one. (In Sydney they are perhaps more likely to be swallowed by a python.) But we are much more likely to come across a venomous spider.

While you may be given a wattle in a pot at your citizenship ceremony, it might be more helpful to receive a guide to the spiders you may encounter in your state. I can still see the first large huntsman I encountered, which immediately brought to mind the tarantula that crawls over Sean Connery's naked shoulder in *Dr No*. If you are used to little cupboard spiders something so large and hairy is disconcerting, even when you know it isn't dangerous. As a child I would fearfully ask my mother to remove daddy long-legs from my bedroom, so I clearly needed to toughen up. You don't need a place in the country to get to know the more venomous varieties, and when I found my first redback in the outside dunny belonging to my first house in Melbourne, I immediately knew what it was because my son had done a spider project in Grade 1. We sent the redback to school with him for 'show and tell', and I realised afterwards that

it should have gone with a trigger warning. It is also possible it went in an inappropriate, insecure shoebox. By the time I had a place in the country the huntsman held no fear for me, which was just as well since most visitors who noticed a large one up near the cornice of the guest bedroom wanted it removed. At certain times of the year, every piece of folded sack or cloth in the shed seemed to be hosting several of them.

By far the most painful experience I had in the country was delivered by an ant – and on more than one occasion. Don Watson declares that ants 'have almost as much claim to iconic status in Australia as the kangaroo or kelpie ... If you are not allergic to its venom, the bite of a bull ant or jack-jumper is a defining bush experience; if you *are* allergic, it may kill you'. I suspect most people meet a bull ant at some point and somehow know to steer clear, as even jumping up and down on them and grinding them under foot does not seem to deter them, only making them really really angry. But I knew nothing about the charmingly named jack-jumper until one bit me. The pain and shock stopped me in my tracks.

A neighbour subsequently pointed out all the little holes in the ground in front of my shed, so that I would recognise the tell-tale signs of their presence. I looked them up and discover they are Tasmania's most deadly creature – their 'killer ant'. The new Tasmanian National Basketball team has just been named the Jack Jumpers, intended to suggest that you can be small but very dangerous. Despite the agony, it is hard to remember to take them seriously. So it did happen again, and I learned to run inside and wash the poison off before applying something numbing to the spot. They were hard to avoid if, like me, you like to garden without gloves.

I am not allergic to jack-jumpers so I didn't die. What did in fact nearly kill me was a segmented worm – a leech. I had noticed the odd one attaching itself to me or my son when he visited and worked in the garden. We knew to get the salt and didn't think much about them. One evening, relaxing in front of the fire, one foot felt a bit damp, so I removed my shoes and that sock. Somewhat to my astonishment my shoe was full of blood – well, that is an exaggeration, but the sock and inside of the shoe were well soaked with it. Baffled, I examined my leg wondering what on earth I could have done, only finding a very small puncture mark where blood was still oozing. These leeches have tiny jaws and teeth with which to bite their 'host', adding an anticoagulant and anaesthetic so you won't realise what they are up to.

After a few days the bottom half of my bitten leg was turning purple and I thought I should check in with my GP. It turned out that I now had cellulitis. It seems that leeches can deposit bacteria from their last few meals into your flesh, especially if you are careless as you remove them. Mine had fallen off of its own accord after a full meal, but still managed to leave something behind. The infection took two weeks to bring under control with extremely powerful antibiotics. I drew round the edge of the purple patch and sent daily photos to my GP so she could monitor its progress. Intrigued about this brush with death, I wondered how to avoid

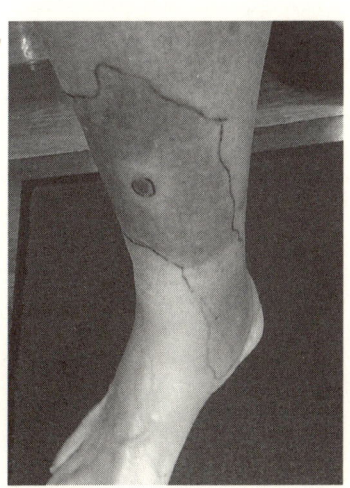

the cause of it. I found out that leeches hang around on the side of plants in the flowerbed just waiting for a blood source to come close enough for them to latch on. A hungry leech is very responsive to light and mechanical stimuli. It tends to change position frequently, and explores its environment by head movement and body waving. It can also assume an 'alert' posture, extending to full length and remaining motionless:

> In response to disturbances by an approaching host [e.g. me], the leech will begin 'inchworm crawling', continuing in a trial and error way until the anterior sucker touches the host and attaches. Aquatic leeches are more likely to display this 'pursuit' behaviour, while common land leeches often accidentally attach to a host.[74]

So now, as well as jack-jumpers, I needed to be on constant alert for leeches as I went around the property. I realised I should probably be wearing gaiters or moleskin pants as protection against these small enemies. While I might feel ridiculous taking such precautions, if anyone raised their eyebrows, I could say I was protecting myself against snakes as I gardened. And I probably should have been, as we have the most venomous snakes in the world on this continent, and a couple of them in my garden.

Perhaps the first Australian snake I got to know was the one confronting the drover's wife, in a Henry Lawson story that is full of fear and dread. I learned useful and interesting things about Victorian snakes when taking the children to Healesville Sanctuary and catching the 'snake show'. In a large room we stood behind a knee-high glass screen, and the snake handlers appeared on the other side with plastic dustbins and snake hooks. Although this was about thirty years ago, I remember discovering that despite their toxicity Australian snakes rarely kill anyone, and that they are extremely useful in dealing with mouse plagues in rural areas. If you stamp your feet as you walk along snakes will make themselves scarce, and only confront you if cornered. And some, while extremely venomous, can't open their jaws wide enough to give you a good bite. As a general rule. Doing a first aid course at work, I learned that contrary to my childhood assumptions, you shouldn't make a tourniquet above the bite to cut off the poison flow, nor cut it open and attempt to suck out the venom. By the time I met my own snake I knew that if bitten you should try to move as little as possible, stay very calm, and wrap a pressure bandage along the bitten limb. You should also take a proper look at the snake so that the right anti-venom can be administered. And your mobile phone will do the rest, if you have signal.

My neighbours advised me that I would most likely see snakes on the move through the garden in summer, as they hunted for water. In the event, my first encounter was finding a tiger snake caught in the netting over the cherry trees, just when the extended family were staying for Christmas. Snakes getting themselves caught in bird netting pinned to the ground over fruit trees, as they tried to pass innocently through in search of water or a mate, turned out to be a fairly regular occurrence. Once the snake's head plus an inch or so of body got through the netting they were unable to reverse out, while also being too big to go forward. I had bought the best-quality bird netting to deal with the bouncing currawongs, and it wasn't going to be torn by a mere snake. The main problem was dealing with the snake once stuck. With a large, enthusiastic dog I couldn't just leave the snake to perish, as she would want to play with it. Friends over the hill in Moggs Creek had lost their glorious golden retriever to snake-bite. On this Christmas occasion my neighbour kindly walked over and blasted the snake's head off with his shotgun. The children were fascinated by the way the snake continued to writhe for several hours after this decapitation.

On the next occasion, when another tiger snake was caught in the netting over the enclosed vegetable garden, I felt I should deal with it myself – after I had shut the dog inside. I learned that it is quite

hard to decapitate a snake with a spade when you can't get a good swing at it. I was sad that it had to die, and in such an undignified way. Afterwards I tried, wherever possible, to tie any netting up off the ground, around the trunks of the apple and plum trees, to minimise the danger to snakes. Apart from the danger they pose to snakes, there is nothing pretty about poly pipe hoops covered in netting dotting the countryside while fruit ripens. I am never reminded of a beautiful French potager or an English walled vegetable garden as I drive about peering into other people's properties. But they don't have bowerbirds and bouncing currawongs to contend with in those countries.

The other occasion I encountered snakes was on sunny mornings when one might be found warming itself up across the driveway, or on a bare patch of earth in the flowerbed next to the front verandah. The first time this occurred I rushed inside to my computer (there being not enough 3G to use my smart phone) to look the snake up so I could work out how alarmed to be. By the time I had decided it was a copperhead and come outside again it had moved somewhere else. The Drover's Wife came back to me, and I did not want the snake settling in. So, I took the torch and crawled under the house to check for signs of home making, just in case.

The most dramatic snake sighting was without danger, however. After some very high winds a substantial branch fell off the largest gum that remained standing inside my garden, a 20-metre-high yellow box. I gazed up the trunk trying to see where the branch had broken off and whether there were any other dangling widow-making branches. I found the spot, a good ten metres up, and there seemed to be a kind of pale green piece of cloth or something caught on the jagged tear. But it was waving vigorously around, despite the wind having dropped. Curious, I went to get my binoculars and was astonished to see a decent-sized snake up there, obviously pinned by tearing wood when the branch broke off, and now trying to wriggle free. Until that point it had never occurred to me that a snake could attack me from above. But I discovered that tiger snakes like to hunt for birds eggs and will climb tall trees to get at them. This one eventually died and then shrank rapidly to nothing – or perhaps an owl ate it before it died. That would have been quite a sight.

Seeing a snake in the garden certainly caused my heart rate to increase, even if – very rarely – it turned out to be a blue-tongued

lizard. But the thought of them going up and down my garden looking for water gives me pleasure. It would give me more pleasure if I had mice to be got rid of, or if they could swallow rabbits like a New South Wales python. Nonetheless I came to feel at home with my snakes and this contributed to my growing sense of belonging in the country, far more than my ant encounters ever did.

Dam, frogs and yabbies

The size of the sky in the country led to me to do uncharacteristic things like get out of bed in the middle of the night to watch an eclipse of the moon. When it is announced that something special is going to happen in the sky at night I am pleased and interested, even if I think twice before setting the alarm. In truth, I forget to look up very much at all. I do, however, go outside every evening after dark to give the dog a chance to relieve herself before I go to bed. On this occasion I have been alerted by my Night Sky app to the fact that conditions for stargazing are 'good' tonight, so I remember to look up. Turning away from the lights of the house, I begin to see hundreds of stars. And then thousands. I don't think the app gets more enthusiastic than 'good'. It doesn't rate any night sky as 'excellent', though that seems a better description right now. 'Fabulous' even. The absence of any city glow and any close neighbours means that, if I turn off the lights in my own house, the sky takes over completely. On a cloudless night, within a short period of time, the sky slowly fills with stars as my eyes adjust to the darkness. It is a miraculous experience, in which everything that is usually chattering away in my head goes quiet, and for some reason it makes me feel intensely alive.

When the sky feels this big finding the Southern Cross seems irrelevant, though at other times I feel that I should be able always to locate it, because of its symbolic and political significance in Australia. Don Watson writes that for settlers 'feeling at home in the Australian bush meant feeling at home not only among the gum trees, but with the Southern Cross sitting in their soul's composition where Ursa Major used to sit'.[75] I have never thought of the stars in the sky as helping me feel that I belong anywhere except on the planet Earth (as opposed to one particular part of it). But this may well be because I have difficulty remembering what star is where and I am also embarrassed to admit this, given the telescope enthusiasm in the family. I can usually find the Southern Cross but I don't feel in any way discombobulated if I can't, only self-conscious if I am with anyone else. After all, what is the Night Sky app for? Which side of the Earth I am on seems singularly insignificant when looking at the stars in these perfect conditions.

My neck begins to hurt as the Milky Way becomes visible to me and I wish I had warmer clothes on so I could lie down and just gaze for a while. I can hear the boobook owl nearby, seeming to call across the valley to a friend who calls back. Such a small and innocent-looking owl, but so ferocious when hunting. Then I remember I have just installed a new app – FrogID – and turn my head in the direction of the dam to listen. There is the usual low chatter that I hear most nights at that time of year, but also the banjo-plucking sound of pobblebonks (which I first thought were more creatures from Edward Lear's imagination), and a sort of light door-knocking sound. I know I should go and test this new app right now given my general lack of enthusiasm for going outside late at night, so I collect a cardigan and my fabulous new torch from Bunnings. I love this torch more than almost any other tool around the house (next to the electric fence voltage tester). It is large, bright green, with four different settings, and can be recharged with a standard USB lead. Most important though, it is so powerful that on a dark night you could find the boobook owl sitting 30 metres up in a gum tree.

I wade through the over-long grass in the paddock towards the dam, the dog accompanying me, but invisible below the seed heads, making waves above her body. The frogs do not seem to mind my approach and continue with their increasingly cacophonous calling. On my phone the app has downloaded a complete directory of all Australian frogs, with photos and other people's recordings of their calls, as well as written descriptions of their size, colouring and pupil shape (if it is horizontal the frog is active in the daytime, if vertical it is active at night). I have not had the foresight to try the app out before this expedition and am praying it is well designed.

It doesn't disappoint, even in the dark. All you have to do is point the phone at the noise and press 'record', and for 60 seconds little darts of yellow shoot out as the timer moves round in a circle, picking up the different types of frog sound. Every five seconds or so there is a longer yellow dart as a loud pobblebonk chimes in. Then it asks me to register the kind of habitat where I am recording (rural, backyard etc) and what kind of water body (pond, river etc). And after processing all this against its data base, it announces that I may have heard eleven different frogs. These are listed in red against the handsome dark blue background of the screen, and it asks me if I agree with its conclusions.

For fear that I may either fall into the dam or trip on the electric fence in my excitement I decide to retreat inside to read up on each of these frogs to see if they match the habitat and likely geographic spread before responding and then submitting the 'My Frogs' record to the Australian Museum. I think that new citizens with children might be presented with this app as frogs can be heard beside almost any body of water, including small urban ponds. I regularly found the little southern brown tree frog in my vegetables, under upturned flower pots and even high up in my raspberry bushes. And if frog health is one of the best indicators of environmental health then this citizen science work really matters.

***

Having a dam feels, in itself, a mark of my Australian-ness. Dams are a ubiquitous feature of the farmed Australian landscape, and they might be thought of as an easily observed barometer, registering variations in local health and happiness. When they are full everyone is happy and there are fewer visits to check the Bureau of Meteorology website. As the water shrinks to the dam's centre, leaving a wider and wider ring of mud or clay, you know people will be talking about the weather and hoping for rain. The damp Otways are about as far away as you could imagine from the western plains of Jill Ker Conway's childhood in New South Wales, but the level of water in the dams is still a regular topic of conversation in summer.

The main purpose of the dam was, of course, to provide water to the paddocks for stock, and to the garden. To water or not, and how much to water, are questions all gardeners ask in most of Australia. My dam was dug by the previous owner when they settled on these paddocks, and it was both large for the acreage and really deep and cold in the centre. It rains a lot in the Otways, but dam water evaporates quickly in hot summers. I had insurance in the form of someone else's irrigation pipe running down the road past my dam, taking water from a spring further up the hill to a eucalypt plantation further down the hill. In exchange for a bottle of single malt whisky I would be able to open the valve to a pipe that led directly to my dam, and let water run into it for a few days.

Neighbours agreed that I could make productive use of the dam itself if I wished – suggesting silver perch, or even trout. But hearing that the perch, if they survived the cormorants, would likely taste 'muddy', and that trout would need logs or big rocks to hide under, yabbies seemed a better option, despite their ability to tunnel through the side walls. And from what I had read about Australian childhoods, yabbying was a quintessential pastime, in Victoria at least. I had even heard of yabbies being seen in the small pond beside the Kew public library, but I had never known how to catch them, let alone how to cook them. I had, however, eaten the West Australian marron in good restaurants in Perth, and fondly imagined myself catching a bucketful of 'freshwater crayfish'. The difference between Victorian yabbies and the marron had to be explained to me, but despite learning that the Victorian crustacean bears no obvious relationship to anything I would call a crayfish, the romance of the yabby remained. I discover there is even a restaurant called Grab a Yabby in Perth, which has only just been rebranded as 'Grabs'.

Asking around I discovered that the 'Queen of Yabbying' lived quite close by. She instructed my son and me to come by one October evening with a couple of buckets, some dried dog food and several yabby nets. We set the yabby traps around the edge of her dam, and the next morning went over and collected probably twenty or thirty to transport to my dam, including a couple that had hundreds of eggs attached to their undersides. I now understood why everyone can go yabbying – all you need is a few bits of dog food and a $10 net. The only constraint was no yabbying in months that did not have an R in them. They tend to be too comatose in the winter months to bother with dog food or even steak.

Walking round the edge of my dam, I never saw any of its new inhabitants, so I was not convinced they had survived. Knowing they grow fast we trapped a few several months later just to reassure ourselves they were still there, and put them in the bath with water so that they could clean themselves. It reminded me of collecting big Roman snails as a child, and putting them in a sawdust bath for the same purpose, before my Francophile parents prepared them for dinner. In the bath I discovered a few floating claws and legs detached from their owners as a result of aggressive encounters in that confined space.

Preparing yabbies to eat is not quite like splitting open a large crayfish. We could have waited a few years for them to get really big, but just fifteen months after releasing our own into the dam, we couldn't resist the idea of a special Christmas dish. Not knowing which bit of the dam they had occupied we spread six nets out around the edge, and the next morning three of them were bulging with catch. It is hard to explain the thrill of this process, from catching them in someone else's dam, releasing them in our dam, and months later catching them again and carrying them back in a red plastic bucket to the house. We ate them for Christmas lunch, sitting out on the deck, with a well-chosen wine. The festive season had never really felt quite right until then, with the heat, the sweating Father Christmases in the city, the fake snow everywhere. That yabby Christmas I don't think I looked back at all. I was settling into this landscape.

Chapter 6
Learning about eucalypts

Australia's city streets are lined with different kinds of trees that tell us a lot about the people who planted them. Some are easy to identify, like the eye-catching jacarandas that were widely planted in the 1920s and 30s for the purposes of civic beautification. Grafton in New South Wales holds an annual jacaranda festival, while tourists flock to the jacaranda tree tunnel on Sydney's north shore and Adelaide promotes its jacaranda flowering season as enthusiastically as Japan promotes its cherry blossom. Once seen in full bloom, they are never forgotten. In more sedate Melbourne it is the glorious elm that rules the major avenues, with the plane tree – often hacked about to protect power lines in ways reminiscent of a French provincial town – a tougher streetfighter to be found all over the city. One of the rarer civic plantings of eucalypts is in the roundabout between Melbourne Cemetery and the University of Melbourne to the north of the city. There a pair of very tall, almost ethereal lemon-scented gums stand in the circle, their glorious smooth pale trunks rising up above the traffic. They give much pleasure and were on the short list for Victorian Tree of the Year in 2016. It is possible that Walter Burley Griffin had them planted there when working on Mannix College for the University of Melbourne.

The Australian tree that is most widely used in streetscapes is the *Melia azedarach*, or white cedar (also called Cape lilac in Perth), one of the very few deciduous trees native to this continent (as well as Southeast Asia). People are often surprised to discover we have such a good-looking deciduous Australian tree. I have planted one in three different suburban Melbourne gardens of mine, though now I have seen a thirty-year-old one in a city neighbour's front garden I wonder about the wisdom of this. They remain small when neglected but can get very big indeed. I also planted one in the country. They have much to recommend them – great shape, charming blossom, beautiful leaves providing dappled shade and pale gold berries.

Choosing urban street trees is a tricky business, and your local council's tree strategy is likely to have a long list of things they have had to take into consideration. There are many potentially noisy voices in local government, some urging the maintenance of traditional streetscapes, some complaining about hay fever or fallen leaves, while others wish to see exotic trees replaced with Australian ones. Street trees have strong evocative powers and it is not hard to imagine the pride with which Melbourne's elms have been viewed since the first plantings in the 1840s. They were selected because they are beautiful and resilient, but also because of the colonists' desire to recreate the familiar urban landscapes of Europe in this unfamiliar continent. There are over 6000 English elms along the city's streets, and over 11 000 are maintained within a 10-kilometre radius of the city centre. As these trees age and their vulnerability increases because of the warming climate, their replacement becomes a topic of much more than horticultural debate. At stake is also the sense of identity among different communities.

Melbourne is perhaps unusually emotionally invested in its trees. In 2012 the City of Melbourne published its Exceptional Tree Register, and then introduced a scheme through which we can email any one of the 60 000 trees within its boundaries and get a reply. The council was taken aback at the depth of feeling expressed in these messages. Sometimes new tree selections bring to the surface tensions between an older settler society and a newer one that wishes to break with the colonial past, as though monarchists were arguing with republicans. Not so long ago a new planting of plane trees down the median strip of the old inner suburb of Carlton led to such protests that they were all dug up and replaced with sugar gums. Clive Blazey, the founder of the Diggers gardening empire, likes to stir the pot on this subject, promoting the use of exotics and complaining that native plants are highly unsuitable in urban environments. He argues that 'we will never establish an Australian garden tradition until our choice of trees is settled', and that eucalypts 'provide lousy shade (their leaves hang down), and the roots poison the soil ... Eucalypts may be extraordinarily beautiful in the bush, but they're not garden-worthy in the city!'[76] In New South Wales the state government is encouraging a similar review of street plantings, with experts arguing that Australian species, such as gum trees, generally have vertical leaves that create open canopies, while deciduous trees, such as maples, liquidamber and plane trees, have horizontal leaves that provide denser shade. On this reasoning deciduous trees should be planted close to homes to reduce urban heat, and native species should be planted in parks and along waterways to provide some shade and habitat for animals and birds.[77]

For Melbourne City Council the focus on trees is also a response to heightened alarm over rising city temperatures, evidence that many older trees are struggling, and the knowledge that it is only going to get warmer. This focus on climate warming is beginning to dominate since many of the much-loved European trees simply cannot cope. The city is widely admired for its Urban Forest Strategy, designed to double the level of tree cover in the city over twenty years of planting. We are going to get more jacarandas, Moreton Bay figs and liquidambers – as well as lemon-scented gums and salmon gums. Other local councils are just as engaged, with Darebin intending to plant 6000 trees in 2021. In one area this council has begun to plant the much less usual bottle tree (*Brachychiton rupestris*) where the pavements are narrow and shop fronts are close to the road. Coming from Queensland originally, these curious-shaped trees will feel much less familiar than a gum tree, let alone an elm. These changes to our urban streetscapes will make the city feel less like home to some and more like home to others. Arguments will no doubt continue, but on balance I am for a focus on cooling, even if that makes me forget where I am.

***

Having complained about the fact that no one could tell me the names of many Australian trees, I knew I was morally obliged to learn to identify more than a handful of the most obvious Victorian eucalypts. My need to know probably reflects a more general personality trait which has only relatively recently made itself visible to me, or more accurately my son made it visible to me. I am always wanting to know what I am looking at, be it a city building, a mountain, a make of car, or a crop in a paddock. I have become one of those tiresome people who can now spend a ridiculous amount of time looking up answers to trivial questions on their phone, or finding new educational apps. Not surprisingly, I felt challenged by gum trees.

Apart from this personality disorder I was focussed on gum trees because I hoped that knowing more about them would change the way I responded to walking or driving through eucalypt woodland. I grew up on the chalky North Downs in Kent, in a house that backed on to a small field and an area of wooded parkland. The big trees we knew were oaks, horse chestnuts and beeches. Not only were these trees radically different from each other in their leaves, bark and form, but each season of the year transformed their appearance dramatically. Inside our garden was a little wood of copper beeches, and just outside in the neighbouring field were some mature ordinary beeches (a tree which is often described as 'stately'). Beech trees are designed for climbing as their branches begin at ground level, stretching out horizontally on a mature tree like the perfect parallel bars. It is not surprising that I found the mountain ash forests east of Melbourne to be disconcertingly one-dimensional, especially after the salmon gums and banksias of Western Australia. And there is no way you can climb a gum tree.

In my country house I armed myself with *Eucalyptus: An Illustrated Guide to Identification*, as well as the very serious two-volume *Flora of the Otway Plain and Ranges*, which reassuringly informed me that

there were not very many different trees in the region. Many of them were surely to be found on my property, or in the nearest bit of protected bush where I often walked my dog. Less intimidating than these volumes, the Victorian Government Information Office also provided detailed maps, and user-friendly coloured brochures with high-quality photographs of the 'Indigenous plants of the Upper Barwon' and the 'Indigenous wildlife of the Upper Barwon'. The former contains a fold-out page on eucalypts with black-and-white drawings of the adult leaf, juvenile leaf, buds and fruit of each, together with a 1-centimetre-high outline of each tree's possible shape. I say 'possible' advisedly, since it seems that the same tree can grow quite differently in different locations. To confuse matters further, to the untrained eye at least, the leaf drawings all looked remarkably alike.

The illustrated guide to identifying eucalypts suggests you start with the bark, and what sounds like a relatively simple question: is it rough or smooth? I think this will be straightforward if I am to be walked through a decision-tree which will take me, after a few selections, to the correct identification. This mood does not last long, however, as on the very next page we are warned that perhaps 'the most difficult character to come to terms with is the bark':

> Most keys require a recognition of smooth or rough [so far so good], then placement of the rough forms into so-called [sic] distinct categories. The easiest to recognise are ironbark, tessellated bark and stringybark, in that order. We simply use 'rough' v. 'smooth', although at the end of one section we resort to an estimation of the approximate amount of rough bark.[78]

This is not sounding so promising. *A Traveller's Fauna*, which I read much later, says that the identification of eucalypts can be complex but agrees the place to start is grouping them into bark types, adding boxes, peppermints, ashes and bloodwoods to iron, tessellated and stringybarks. I move on, in hope, to the defining issue of 'bud clusters', since I have long been led to believe that this is the most definitive key. But here too there is an immediate 'note of caution' about bud numbers (which come in the categories of 'single', 'threes', 'sevens', or 'more than sevens' – up to more than fifty). Put simply, buds can fall or be knocked off, and to be confident of the real number you would need to look for the scars left by fallen buds. So, in order to use the bud key you should start with the numbers of buds (and scars), and then within the relevant numbers, divide the tree into the further category choice of 'tree' or 'mallee'. Then you look at the position of the buds, the bark type (see above) and the fruit size. After you have done all this, 'when numbers of species become manageable, final consultation is to be made by seeing all the confirmatory information in the digests, including the natural distribution'.[79] All perfectly clear so far?

Eucalyptus viminalis, the manna gum, is my first (and only) doubt-free identification. You can't really miss them as they are enormous and their older bark peels off in great strips, leaving the most beautiful pale grey and pink new bark underneath. They line the road to my property and are dotted around the edges of the paddocks, often with long strips of bark lying across the electric fences, threatening to short the circuit by squishing one wire against the next. I don't need to look at the buds.

A neighbour told me that she has heard the grunting or snoring noise made by a male koala (as opposed to the high-pitched wailing cry of a female) in the vicinity of my house. Somewhat sceptically I looked up koala habitats and discover that they are particularly fond of the leaves of the manna gum. So I did spend some time gazing upward into my manna gums, and also down at their feet looking for

the characteristic dry green-brown pellets I should find there – but without success. There is something special about finding a koala in the wild, unless you live near Cape Otway, where an 'over-abundance' has resulted from 'their love of Manna gums, reluctance to change food source, favourable climatic conditions and an absence of predators'.[80] The result is almost leafless trees. For me the prospect remained exciting, but unlikely in my area. However, late one evening I was driving back after dinner with friends in Aireys Inlet, over the unsealed road that runs through the Otway national park. I always had an eye out on this road for a kangaroo or black wallaby that might jump in front of me, or a rabbit that I might attempt to run over. On this occasion I noticed a pair of eyes to one side of the road, reflected in my headlights. After slowing to drive safely past I realised the eyes were too low to be a kangaroo and too high to be a rabbit. Intrigued, I braked and then cautiously backed up the road to where I had seen them. In doing so I almost ran over a large koala making very slow progress across the road. I got out, distinctly excited, and watched for a few minutes. Then I thought I should make sure it got across the road safely in case another vehicle came this way. It didn't seem to mind my herding attempts, and I realised that it was in fact wearing a large radio transmitter round its neck. While this reduced my sense of wonderment, I nevertheless felt pleased with myself for having seen a koala in 'the wild', even if it was clearly part of a rehabilitation program.

Information about the natural distribution of different trees looks to me like the one really useful tool if you are looking for a shortcut to identification. My glossy brochure on what is to be found in the Upper Barwon makes the odds of correctly guessing any particular local tree pretty good. It alerts me to likely sightings of river red gums, blue gums, or snow gums, which I will probably recognise if they are big enough. (There is, in fact, a large blue gum plantation a little further up the hill, but that is not what I want to see.) Much more problematic are brown stringybark (*Eucalyptus baxteri*), swamp gum (*Eucalyptus ovate*) and the yarra gum (*Eucalyptus yarraensis*), all of which seem to have seven buds and rough bark. I am not even confident I will recognise a narrow-leaved peppermint gum (*Eucalyptus radiata*), which has at least seven buds. The Vicflora website tells me its bark is rough and fibrous, the leaves are particularly narrow (as are the leaves of all peppermint gums), and that I can hope to find some that will give themselves away by smelling particularly pepperminty.

While I am not sure I will be able to tell one tree from another, I am learning a lot about eucalypts from this preparatory reading. I write brief notes about the identifying characteristics (if you could call them that) of each eucalypt that I might expect to find on my block of land, and on a cool morning head out round the property to collect leaves and buds or nuts (being unsure which tree flowers when). I have my secateurs to cut off small branches with buds, flowers or fruits on them, and a pencil for bark rubbing. My phone is also ready to capture bark characteristics.

To cut a long story short, I think that going to live in the country has not increased my ability to recognise different eucalypts by much, although it has certainly increased my general understanding of the genus as a whole. Really, I failed. I am not sure if this is because I did not try hard enough and/or I left it too late in life and my grey cells couldn't cope. But, in my defence, I am prepared to argue that eucalypt identification is objectively difficult. I later discover that there are 800 eucalypt species, and they are constantly hybridising.[81] Reading Don Watson I learn that 'identifying Australian plants presents unique difficulties because of their habits of "promiscuous intercourse"' – the very thing that makes eucalypts 'so adaptable and enduring'.[82] At that point I cease to beat myself up about my failure, and stop thinking it is strange that so few Australians can tell one gum from another.

I planted tiny tubes of the swamp and yarra gums in the paddock to the east of my garden, hoping they would help to connect the house to the bush beyond. If I had stayed there long enough I might have had my own Upper Barwon arboretum and would probably have got the hang of them. But really my larger gain in understanding and interest is from Tim Low's descriptions as he illuminates the relationship between our uniquely noisy birds and eucalypts. I feel differently about the mountain ash when he tells me that a single *Eucalyptus regnans* 'can throw out a million flowers in one season and a thousand flames the next'.[83] Or that 'Blue gum flowers are so large the nectar can be swilled around in them'.[84] Or that eucalypts produce such overwhelming amounts of sugar in their tree sap that sap-sucking bugs have to 'imbibe more sap than they need in order to get their protein needs, so excess flows from their anuses as honeydew or is sculpted into lerp palaces, often looking like limpets in clusters'.[85] This is much more interesting than counting gumnuts.

Once I had made a bit of an effort with gum trees, I returned to the question of why this seems to matter to me. At one level the answer is obvious. Eucalypts dominate the Australian landscape in a way that no one tree does in England. The shape of them against the sky is instantly recognisable. In my early years in Australia I used to find

the irregular shape of most eucalypts, and the common occurrence of dead branches, disconcerting, or just untidy or straggly, perhaps because I read this as meaning the trees were unhealthy or dying. I am now well past that stage of feeling out of kilter with the landscape, and in certain kinds of light, they can now give me the kind of happy pang that a horse chestnut in flower used to do.

The eucalypt is not only everywhere on the horizon, it is also everywhere in the cultural landscape – from the swagman's 'coolibah tree' to the one where the kookaburra sits with his pants on fire; from Albert Namatjira's renderings of the ghost gums of central Australia, with their memorable luminous white trunks, to Grace Cossington Smith's treed Turramurra landscapes. I have never been to the McConnell Ranges where Namatjira painted, but I feel I might have from his pictures. Not long after I arrived in Western Australia someone showed me how to whistle with a gum leaf (though I have not noticed anyone doing it since), and the song 'Home Among the Gum Trees' had just been written for a contest to find a new national

anthem. Today Woolworths promotes its sales of Ecostore laundry liquid as 'Fragranced with nostalgic eucalypt'. And Australians abroad speak wistfully about the smell and sound of dry gum leaves under foot. For my mother's eightieth birthday I bought three big framed colour photographs of eucalypt trunks from the photographer Bill Bachman. They are almost abstract and seem too beautiful to be real. They now hang on the wall of my younger brother's house in Brittany, where probably nobody realises they are in fact trees because no French tree looks like that.

Fortunately, feeling at home among the gum trees does not require deep or even wide knowledge. But I learned enough to make me realise I should know more. Living close to large gums caused me to read up on their habit of shedding limbs, and the competing claims about which is the best widow-maker – the scribbly gum, the lemon-scented gum, the river red gum, or the ghost gum, that is reported as having a particular set against timber workers. When I first owned the property I would often park my car in under the spreading branches of a couple of manna gums beside my large shed, to shade it from the sun. One afternoon a huge branch came smashing down on to the shed, a metre from my car. There is no danger now of me ever pitching a tent under any eucalypt, or leaving my car under one either. From time to time a great tearing sound from the other side of the paddocks alerted me to new branch falls. Major rainfall made it highly possible that some great tree would fall across the road, and everyone else along my ridge drove out with a chainsaw in the back when the rain was of the earth-loosening kind. Seeing one blocking the narrow road brought home the real risk that a fallen tree could shut me in with an advancing fire. That evening I went online and ordered two woollen fire blankets to keep in the car in case I should get caught trying to leave.

Fire planning

Living close to pieces of remnant bush, where large stands of eucalypts still line some stretches of road and the gullies, focusses the mind on fire. I absorbed many lessons from reading Robert Kenny's memoir and Tom Griffiths' warnings, but I also learned by burning things, especially eucalyptus leaves. Like everyone else I always had a bonfire being built in at least one paddock. On my pile there were nearly always branches that have fallen off the gum trees, or that have been cut away to open up views, as well as prunings from the shrubby melaleucas along the windbreak, and long strips of peeled bark. One spring, well before the fire ban season, there is a very large pile needing to be burned after some serious tidying-up around the paddock fences, and along the roadside. A low-wind day while the grass is still green and damp provides perfect conditions, and we take rakes and forks out to the pile along with some newspaper and firelighters. The fire takes hold easily and within a very short time the pile is ablaze, with flames leaping much higher into the sky than I anticipated. The crackling and roaring noises immediately remind me of the accounts of bushfire survivors, as does the black smoke. The ferocity of the fire pushes us back, and even though the grass is green we fill the buckets we have brought with water from the cattle trough, just in case something in the paddock catches. It is both a wonderful but also frightening sight.

A year later I have a couple of small piles of dead wood tidied up from around one of the other paddocks, and decide they need burning. This year the winter has been much dryer and while it is still early spring the grass is short and more brown than green. Barely have I lit the first pile when I can see embers settling into the short dry grass and causing it to glow red. I have buckets and there is a trough nearby, but I realise I need to stay close until it has all burned and I can put the fire out completely. I collect a garden chair and a book and settle in for an afternoon keeping watch. I am suddenly reminded that my mother was quite well known when we were young for lighting a large autumn bonfire in our garden, and it escaping far enough for the fire brigade to be called. This was not a usual occurrence on the North Downs.

The following Christmas, at the local fireguard meeting held two properties down the road, the Country Fire Authority (CFA) have brought a fire truck along to show they mean business. Long metal tables have been set up, on which have been laid out some large strips of hessian, with small rocks arranged under it to create a series of miniature hills and valleys. And strewn along the hessian are different kinds of plant material. We gather around the table and watch a surprisingly enlightening demonstration of how fires along our ridge are likely to burn. Using some kind of accelerant on different parts of the hessian, we can see how much faster flames move up a 'hill' than across flat country, and how easily eucalypt and acacia burn compared to oak or viburnum. I feel that this is exactly what Tom

Griffiths means when he asks that we 'empower local residents and their knowledge of local ecologies'.[86]

Meanwhile I have had the fire pump on the dam serviced and cleared away the fallen leaves near the house. I have left the two beautiful Japanese maples close to the house as some people argue that they are effective in catching embers as well as being slow-ish to burn. All round the house are a series of irrigated lawns that stay green through summer, and there are hoses able to wet the house and verandah on severe fire danger days. I feel very different about fire from my first summer, no longer leaving on every single severe fire warning day. I have filled in the CFA self-diagnostic questionnaire to determine how fire-ready I am, and have worked out where my shelter of last resort is. I don't plan to stay and defend, but I am at the same time not frightened of getting caught and being unable to leave.

Chapter 7
The road out of the city

Getting to know one small bit of the country could be expected to help with my feelings of unease about the Australian landscape, or at least create a sense of familiarity with one part of this enormous continent. Looking back, it seems a bit extreme to buy 28 acres for this purpose. I could have joined the Friends of Merri Creek or Darebin Parklands Association or something similar. I now know that Darebin Parklands has 80 acres of restored bushland reserve, only 9 kilometres from the Bourke St Mall. Park rangers will take you on wildlife spotlighting walks, or you can fish with professional instructors, and young people can apply to camp out there overnight. The Merri Creek may not sound like much, but it cuts through the heart of Melbourne from north to south until it joins the Yarra, at Dights Falls in Abbotsford. A lot goes on along this waterway, and thanks to the Friends of Merri Creek there are now fewer plastic bags and more ducks, and even the occasional platypus sighting. On one occasion, just in front of my startled car, a deer bounded up on to the bridge on High St that crosses the waterway as it flows between Northcote and Clifton Hill. The deer crossed the bridge before heading back to the green corridor along the creek. Deer are a pest and should be shot, but its presence reminded me that there is a lot of bush in the city.

There was a time when I was charmed by the distinctive sound of a bellbird on the city outskirts, for its sound is almost as iconic as the kookaburra's laugh. From a sailing ship approaching Australia Mark Twain, no less, reported a young naturalist's description of 'the creature that at short intervals all day rings out its mellow and exquisite peal from the deeps of the forest'.[87] The naturalist is rather obviously relying on a famous poem which appeared in the Sydney Morning Herald in 1867, by Henry Kendall. I am reliably informed that for much of the 20th century most Australians would have known and loved this poem about bellbirds in their cool forest homes, 'down the dim gorges', 'where moss and the sedges/Touch with their beauty the banks and the ledges.' In summer the 'silver-voiced' bell birds guide thirsty wayfarers 'to spring and to river'.

> And, softer than slumber, and sweeter than singing,
> The notes of the bell-birds are running and ringing.

Contemporary bird watchers have a more jaundiced view of this sound, suggesting that it can drive you mad if you have to live near it. Saturating their environment with song (noise) is one way bellbirds eliminate the competition for food, and that is why you are unlikely to hear any other birdsong where they have taken up residence.

Now when I hear a bellbird I am no longer charmed. I have learned that they are enormously destructive of forest trees, causing them to sicken and eventually die because of their love of lerp, the honeydew secreted by the bugs (psyllids) living in the eucalypts. These birds evolved a strategy to protect the source of their lerp, aggressively driving off any other birds who might wish to eat those bugs. The bugs proliferate in this cosseted environment, offering up ever larger quantities of lerp to the bellbirds, but also eating the leaves of the host tree until there are none left, and the tree dies. Bell miners, to give them their less romantic name, are now culled in Victoria.[88] I did not need to leave town to observe all this.

But my goal was not to embed myself in a piece of natural bush nor to create a garden of indigenous plants. I want to understand the landscapes through which I drive, with all their history of dispossession, clearing and felling and grazing and planting, as well as remnant 'nature'. I want to feel more at home in 'the bush' the way Don Watson defines it:

> Collapsing into a single word or image tropical rainforest and mulga, and all the ecosystems in between, is a natural enough convenience, but the bush describes much more than vegetation and native creatures ... It has equal measures of what was there before Europeans came and what is there now. It is what we have done to the natural environment and what it has done to us. The world outside us and the world within.[89]

Perhaps no one can feel at home in all of it. When George Seddon landed in Perth from Victoria, he admits he was ill-prepared, and really didn't like Western Australia. 'The country was all wrong ... where were the ferntree gullies, the high plains, the trout? All the plants scratched your legs. The jarrah was a grotesque parody of a tree, gaunt, misshapen, usually with a few dead limbs, fire-blackened trunk, and barely enough leaves to shade a small ant.'[90] It slowly dawned on him that he wasn't an Australian at all, but a Victorian.

It is possible that all I have managed to become so far is a Victorian, and even this sense of belonging is tested when I drive through the countryside trying to make sense of what I see out of the window. The trip from Melbourne to Deans Marsh is hard to love, at least until you get past Geelong on the Princes Highway and cut through Ceres and then head south and west along the Cape Otway Road. (And while we are here, how come the most important road in Australia, running from Sydney to Adelaide, is still named after the Duke of Windsor?) When I ask friends who make the drive regularly what they would say is the most interesting thing they see en route, I get mostly silence. But someone comes up with the moment on the freeway when you can count on seeing pelicans flying across overhead, going to and from the sewage plant at Werribee. The pelican is indeed a miraculous bird to the northern European eye, and yes, it is a highlight in my book too. On the Princes Highway the most dramatic (as opposed to interesting) thing you are likely to see is acid-yellow fields of flowering canola in September and October. International students pull over with their smart phones, while Tripadvisor issues strong warnings against walking into the fields and damaging the crop in the quest for more dramatic photo opportunities. They are indeed an eye-popping sight, but they also remind me of driving past the vast Monsanto plant at Soda Springs in remote Idaho. Is this Roundup Ready canola planting, I always wonder?

The only other striking thing you see before Geelong, and it is striking only in a relative sense, are the You Yangs – what from the road look like two little hills sitting in the flat Werribee Plain. They do not look enticing enough to get me off the freeway no matter how often I drive this route. That is, until I go and see the exhibition of Fred Williams' paintings of these little hills at the Geelong Gallery in 2017. I am taken aback to learn how often he painted these granite outcrops, and how important these works were in the development of his unique interpretations of the Australian landscape. Williams tells us that when he came back to Australia after five years painting the human figure in London, 'I looked at the landscape and I did see that there was something that I wanted to say. It became obsessive with me'. The You Yangs paintings are essentially abstract and yet immediately recognisable, especially once his radical insight is explained. 'In Australia there is no focal point. Obviously, it was too good a thing for me to pass up. If there's going to be no focal point in a landscape, then it had to build into paint.'[91]

It is hard to argue with the insight that there is no focal point in the You Yangs, but Fred Williams' paintings nonetheless make you want to go there. They tell you not to look for anything picturesque, not to expect drama of any kind, and there is no concession to conventional perspective. 'The space is flattened and tilted towards the viewer, implying a microcosmic as well as an aerial viewpoint'; 'the trees ... don't grow out of the hillside. They are part of it'.[92] The rocks and trees appear as dots and dabs of paint, not sitting on the land but integrated into it, and often there is no horizon to distract the eye. An altogether ordinary landscape has been endowed with something magical because a painter has transformed the way we see it, bringing an intense simplicity and clarification to the image. The paintings are beautiful because of their formal design and the application of the paint itself, not because they reproduce something of obvious beauty. They change what we see in a powerful act of imaginative apprehension.

Friends who drive up and down to Geelong struggled to suggest any other notable sights from the road, apart from the relentless creep of new houses along the route. No-one has gone off piste to explore the Brisbane Ranges which can be seen in the distance, north of Geelong. Perhaps this is the tyranny of distance, as it is hard to imagine anyone 'dawdling through the countryside' when it is so far between sights and journeys are often already long. This regular two-hour road trip to my country house drives me into the arms of Audible and I manage the whole of Proust's *In Search of Lost Time* in my first year, followed by Anthony Powell's *A Dance to the Music of Time* in the second. I am eager to get in the car every time.

A few years after I started going up and down, I noticed the appearance of a new sign on the freeway at Werribee announcing 'You are now entering Wadawarrung Country'. Twenty-two Welcome to Country signs were erected across Western Victoria's arterial road network in 2015 as a State Labor Government initiative to recognise the traditional owners of the land through which these roads pass. From the Fred Williams exhibition I learned that the You Yangs range is an ancient site in Wathaurong Country and specific to the Yaawangi clan group, and that it remains a place of great significance to its traditional owners. In these ridges can be found evidence of Indigenous water gathering and the storing of water in wells. The Wathaurong Aboriginal Cooperative works on maintaining both the natural and cultural heritage of the You Yangs.

I am embarrassed by how little I knew. I had read Richard Broome's *Aboriginal Victorians*, but it felt more like a duty than a revelation. It wasn't until I read Bruce Pascoe's 2014 book *Dark Emu: Aboriginal Australia and the Birth of Agriculture* that I began to see the lived history of Victoria's Indigenous population as something that I could relate to directly. Pascoe made it possible to imagine Aboriginal families and clans living in this landscape, doing exactly what we are still doing and that all human societies do, namely managing the land and water to ensure a reliable and varied diet for themselves. As for those boring flat dun-coloured paddocks between the freeway and the You Yangs, it turns out they contain a designated 15 000-hectare grassland reserve, intended to protect the tiny amount of the original ecosystem that remains on Wathaurong country. A report in the *Age* newspaper suggests, plausibly, that 'It's quite possible many Victorians have never seen a healthy grassland ecosystem. They're among the most critically endangered habitats in Australia, and only 1 per cent of the original covering remains'.[93] One of the reasons is that, as Bruce Pascoe points out, grasslands have an image problem. 'They're not terribly sexy. People love forests and stuff like that, but grasslands are really important.'[94]

Some people may be drawn into the grasslands by a love of the small plants growing on them – the tall, fast-growing spears of native grasses interspersed with lilies, daisies and other native herbs. But this probably requires some previously acquired enthusiasm for botany. What I think is more likely to help most of us understand and perhaps care about these grasslands is being able to picture Aboriginal women collecting and storing grass seeds and at the same time creating a carefully controlled cultural landscape, in which 'mosaic burning was used to regenerate native grasses and maintain open plains that attracted grazing animals such as kangaroos'.[95]

This landscape, historically managed by Indigenous people, is not just sitting there waiting to be noticed. Most of it has been erased by the activities of sheep and humans. But with luck no Australian schoolchild will any longer be learning that Aboriginal Australians were simply hunter-gatherers, foraging and hunting for their food. What Pascoe has shown us is evidence of people:

> building dams and wells; planting, irrigating, and harvesting seed; preserving the surplus and storing it in houses, sheds or secure vessels; and creating cemeteries and manipulating the landscape – none of which fitted the definition of a hunter-gatherer.[96]

As Melbourne has spread outwards the paddocks beside the freeway have been built over with large house/tiny garden housing estates, and the traffic is now nearly always heavy, everyone travelling a little too close together at 103 kilometres an hour, with a touch of the brakes for the speed cameras at Little River. Geelong has also been creeping over the hills towards its bypass so that there is not a lot of country to see. Beyond Geelong the remaining traffic mostly peels off to the surf coast, leaving only a handful of vehicles pushing on to the west – to Winchelsea, Colac and the Western District – on a freeway that seems to have been built for votes in a marginal federal seat rather than to manage traffic.

To get to my place I usually turned off on the Cape Otway Road and then on to the Winchelsea-Deans Marsh Road, heading south-west and then south. To the south the low hills of the Otways appear, running between me and the sea, and finally the road finds itself bending its way between tall stands of remnant bush. Over the trips back and forth I begin to recognise the wattles and gums of the region – the big blackwoods and manna gums as well as the prickly sweet bursaria when it is covered in little white flowers.

Nearly everyone will have at some point driven along a road where local eucalypts of a mature age still stand on either side – in Western Australia it might be through tall karri trees in the south west, or the wandoo gums along the road to York, or the startling shiny trunks of salmon and gimlet gums out in the wheatbelt. When the sun shines through the open canopy of a roadside stretch of mature gum trees, often with scrappy bark and always with dangling leaves, I feel as glad as I could feel driving through the treed roads of England or France. Is this, in part, because the distressing extent of tree-clearing in Australia, which continues at world record levels today, is almost always visible in the landscape, so that even a brief experience of narrow woodland from a car brings happiness?[97]

On the little unsealed back road to Aireys Inlet the dominant eucalypt changes three times in the space of twenty minutes, from the great, peeling manna gums to snow gums, and finally to the red ironbarks (*Eucalyptus tricarpa*) with their dark fissured trunks as you descend to the coast. I don't need a horse chestnut any more, though I will always love them. I keep a guide to eucalypts in the car, just in case I start to feel adrift.

Chapter 8
Enlarging my horizons to the west

Victoria is a small, relatively well-populated state by Australian standards. But to most immigrants it must feel quite big and pretty empty. The population is heavily concentrated in Melbourne and Geelong to the south, with the much smaller cities of Bendigo and Ballarat to the north. When hundreds of thousands of Melbournians pour out of the city on a long weekend they are overwhelmingly headed for the coast, whether that is Phillip Island and Wilson's Promontory to the east or Torquay and Lorne to the west. At the beach they are unlikely to notice the latitude (and that they are in southern Spain rather than Provence), and in any case the water is always really cold, which is confusing. Along the coastline, native vegetation has been protected, even if in places these are rather thin strips. The coastal tea tree (*Leptospermum laevigatum*) is perhaps the other instantly recognisable indigenous plant for Victorians, along with the gum and the wattle. The winds bend its rough trunks into shapes worthy of Japanese bonsai. It is a plant that is easy to love as it tunnels you on to the beach or accompanies you waist-high along the cliff top in wind-groomed neatness.

The coast all the way west to Portland struggles under the sheer number of tourists who visit briefly each year, and the holiday-makers who stay for two weeks in the summer if they are lucky. You can drive your visitors from overseas along this shoreline and there will be no need to explain why you have taken this long trip. By contrast, there are relatively few compelling reasons for most Victorians to drive more directly west across the state to Hamilton or Horsham, Warracknabeal or Nhill. Thousands of Australians went to see the award-winning movie *Road to Nhill*, but I doubt any of them went there as a result. If they had, about three and half hours from Melbourne they would have passed, on their left, a series of five spectacular sandstone ridges rearing up out of the ground, running north to south. What makes the Grampians such a memorable sight is that the eastern side of each ridge is steep and craggy while the western side slopes more gently. Driving past these ridges on the road through Dunkeld to the south, they run alongside you like giant saw-tooth eruptions on the otherwise flat landscape. They are worth the drive just to look at from a distance. But Gariwerd, the Grampians National Park, is also home to the largest number of significant and ancient Aboriginal rock art paintings and shelters in southern Australia. There is a human as well as a geological history here.

Like most Victorians I had no reason to travel west inland, beyond endlessly planning to visit the Grampians during the wildflower season and always finding it had just finished and school holidays had just started – so putting it off until the next year. But I have driven back and forth past them many times over the last decade, having managed to finally wheedle my way into the affections of someone who is now the third generation of her family running a sheep and cattle property near Casterton in the Western District. (She might just as easily have come from a family growing wheat and lentils in the Wimmera, or milking cows in Gippsland, in which case my knowledge of and familiarity with the Victorian landscape would have been different.) I already knew people with beach houses and bush houses but once the children no longer needed to be taken

on holiday I had no particular desire to be in those places beyond appreciating the opportunity to visit. What I had been missing was a way into what in England I would have called 'country life'.

It was my good fortune to find friendship in the pastoral industry as opposed to dairy or cropping, as it took me across and around the Western District (which I rapidly learned was singular not plural, despite its size). Sometimes I would drive from Deans Marsh, via Colac and Camperdown, and sometimes from Melbourne, via Ballarat cross country to Glenthompson, or Ballarat to Ararat and then south, with all routes meeting at Hamilton to continue west on the Glenelg Highway. From a European perspective the first thing to say about this drive is that it is overwhelmingly flat and also long. Having driven across the Nullarbor a few times, and from Melbourne to Noosa and back, I know there are longer drives. But still, in Europe you could get from Paris to Brussels, Milan to Nice, or from Berlin to Prague for fewer kilometres. And it has to be admitted there would be more to see along the way. Moreover, what there is to see in the west of Victoria would not, I think, be obviously intelligible to an immigrant from Europe, or Vietnam or India.

The western plains are mostly very flat, but dotted with cones and craters caused by volcanic activity ranging from 5 million years ago to 5000 years ago. This is also the reason for their rich soils. You might not notice the rich soils driving through, but you will certainly notice the scoria cones. Sitting on the flat plains these cones are often visible from a long way away. When I first saw them they seemed so unnatural that I thought they must be tailings from some local mining operation, a pale imitation of the Phoenix gold mine tailings in Norseman. Depending on my route to Casterton I go past several and on one occasion, detouring to look for a country pub particularly well regarded for its food, I went past the aptly named Mount Elephant, one of the highest at about 250 metres – or 380 metres if Wikipedia is right. It erupted about 180 000 years ago, and has a hidden crater reaching 120 metres down into the pile of scoria that was built up by volcanic activity. I should drop in if I can arrange to be going past on a Sunday afternoon as it seems there is a visitor centre with nature displays and light refreshments, staffed once a week by local volunteers to answer questions. [98]

What attracted the attention of the first colonial explorer who traversed the Western District in 1836 was not the cones and craters but the broad sunlit grasslands around them, stretching to the horizon. In Don Watson's account, Major Thomas Livingstone Mitchell reported that he had found 'this Eden', 'ready for the immediate reception of civilized man'. 'Gold with breast high kangaroo grass', the 'most fattening grass', 'full and ripe and waving in the wind, it had lain waiting in the swelter of the sunlight'.[99] Heading south-west from Casterton, Mitchell found that the Henty family had already discovered *Australia Felix*, having landed in Portland Bay two years earlier and begun the settlement of the land that was to be called Victoria.[100] After Mitchell's glowing account of the district was published, many more Britons were prepared to invest and settle there. In 1837 a contemporary account describes how a fleet of fifteen or twenty small ships 'each carrying from 300 to 1000 sheep ... [was] employed in conveying stock from the Tamar to Geelong from January to the middle of May'.[101] By the mid-1840s, Margaret Kiddle tells us, 'there were only forty-four runs in Gippsland compared with 282 in the rich Western District which was closer settled than any other part of the new land'.[102] Still, not exactly close by European standards, with properties often covering around 100 000 acres. The Hentys are famous for their sheep (at the Merino Downs homestead), but it has also been suggested that the land around Lake Bolac and Streatham is some of the best land in the world for growing crops.[103]

We know a great deal about the enthusiasm with which news of the pastoral potential of the Western District spread, thanks to Margaret Kiddle's classic history of the region. It did not take long for the Scots to start arriving, 'who were the spearhead of middle-class emigration to the other side of the world; first to Van Diemen's Land, and then to the country which was to become the Western District of Victoria'. Within a decade substantial bluestone houses were being built across the countryside. Within two decades the Manifold family were commissioning Eugene von Guerard to paint a delightful pair of 'portraits' of 'Purrumbete', their homestead near Camperdown. One painting looks out from the verandah across the lake, while the other, *Purumbeete from Across the Lake*, shows us the homestead, with Mount Elephant in the distance.

The Manifolds had become very rich almost overnight when the price paid for mutton and beef shot up because of the influx of gold-diggers after that precious metal was discovered near Ballarat in 1851. With somewhere between 8000 to 10 000 head on Purrumbete, the value of the property quadrupled.[104] The price of wool may have had its ups and downs, but it too contributed to the prosperity of these settlers. In 1873 a major pastoralist reported that sheep men were 'wallowing in wealth not knowing what to do with their income'.[105] Four pastoralists were reckoned to own over one million sheep each.[106] As can be seen from Harriet Edquist's collection of photographs of 19th century Western District houses, they got grander and grander.[107]

The notion that the western plains were 'natural grasslands' lying 'waiting' for the arrival of British settlers has now been thoroughly upended. Just as I was about to buy my bit of the Otways, historian Bill Gammage published his influential account of how those grassy plains and lightly timbered hills had in fact been created by Aboriginal land management techniques, in *The Biggest Estate on Earth: How Aborigines Made Australia*.[108] It is now not uncommon to hear discussion of Indigenous approaches to burning off the land, and the potential for 'cold burns' as opposed to settler 'hot burning' to help us manage not only grasslands, but to reduce the threat of bushfires.

In his introduction to the book, historian Henry Reynolds argues that Gammage's achievement is not just a literary one:

> He is able in a unique way to see the landscape historically: to read it back to what it was like in the past. Anyone who has shared a journey across any part of Australia with Bill will return with intimations about the possibility of seeing the country in a totally new way.[109]

Bill Gammage certainly changed the way I see the landscape as I drive across the state, or at least how I try to see and reimagine the landscape. This requires effort and does not come easily, both because the Indigenous people have been removed from view, and the land has been transformed by the pastoral industry over the past 190 years. An act of imagination is needed because little cultural memory remains of the old landscape. As one reviewer put it:

> many of its diverse plants, animals, flowers and even colours and sounds have been forgotten. This absence has facilitated the persistence of a mythology that first settlers found the continent barren and ugly. In fact, the most common terminology early Britons employed represented the highest praise of an Englishman: the grasslands were *park*-like. By this was

> not meant a national park, but a gentleman's park or estate, in which large trees were carefully situated within pampered grassland, providing sustenance and shelter to an array of grazing animals.[110]

It is hard to look at a sheep in a paddock the same way after reading about their impact on the soils and plants of this continent. Gammage gives us a contemporary account by John Robertson of the changes that were wrought to the grasslands in Wannon (west of Hamilton on the road to Coleraine and Casterton) between 1840 and his return visit in 1853. It is painful to read. Robertson can see that the sheep have already destroyed the indigenous herbaceous plants and strong tussocky grasses which held the soil together:

> The clay is left perfectly bare in summer. The strong clay cracks; the winter rain washes out the clay; now mostly every little gully has a deep rut; when rain falls it … rushes down these ruts … carrying earth, trees, and all before it … Ruts seven, eight, and ten feet deep, and as wide, are found for miles, where two years ago it was covered with a tussocky grass like a land marsh.[111]

Perhaps the most memorable words on the cause of this loss of vegetative cover and topsoil, and the creation of irreversible desert, are provided by George Seddon:

> Looking up from the ground, a sheep is four little mobile jackhammers, pounding to dust the thin skin of an old land that had known only the gentler limbs of the kangaroo.[112]

Elsewhere he has explained how it is that in Europe, indigenous flora can survive beside agricultural and introduced species, but in Australia, indigenous flora rarely survive competition from introduced species where the ground has been disturbed.[113] The fragility of Australian flora is hard to see without it being explained. Charles Massy took over the management of his family's merino and cattle property near Cooma in New South Wales in the 1980s. In his influential book *The Cry of the Reed Warbler*, he presents powerful arguments about the need for new approaches to farming, but he begins by acknowledging how ignorant he was despite growing up on this land. 'And yet, though intimately my country, I came to realise that for a long time I didn't fully understand it. Consequently, at times, I caused immense damage to this country – in some paddocks, perhaps at least a few thousand years worth.'[114]

How we see and understand the environment is actively shaped by art and the humanities as much as an understanding of botany, geology or farming, and for a lot of us art or even poetry is going to have a bigger impact than science. The poems of Banjo Patterson and Dorothea McKellar gave us words and images about our 'sunburnt country' and the 'shade of the Coolibah tree' that we all recognise. So it is not surprising that writers like Bill Gammage, George Seddon and Don Watson want to make us think critically about how some of Australia's most loved artists have mythologised the landscape in the paintings that we love most. They are as one in their decision to pick on Arthur Streeton, someone whose work I was introduced to in just the kind of exhibition that these writers want to deconstruct. In 1985, four years after I had landed in Melbourne, the NGV presented one of its most popular exhibitions of Australian paintings, called *Golden Summers: Heidelberg and Beyond*. I had just become a citizen and had a one-year-old Australian daughter. I loved it. The title of the exhibition was taken from one of Streeton's most famous paintings, *Golden Summer, Eaglemont* (1889). Twenty years later the Geelong Gallery presented an exhibition of Streeton's post-war paintings of the Western District, focused around his *Land of the Golden Fleece* (1926), by which time I was ready to think and feel differently about Streeton's landscapes.

In his review of the Geelong exhibition for the *Sydney Morning Herald*, John McDonald describes the signature picture:

> The painting looks out across a sun-raked plain towards Mount William in the Grampians. It is the definition of the classic blue-and-gold Aussie landscape. The sparse gum trees, the flock of sheep, the bleached grass and long shadows that intrude from the left are all calculated to twang on Australian heartstrings. The blue form of Mount William presides over the scene like an immensely old, worn Olympus, from which the fickle Gods have long since departed. It's a portrait of a peaceful, pastoral land.[115]

There are three versions of this painting, and the curator's note about the one that is owned by the National Gallery of Australia in Canberra alerts the visitor to the possibility that this is more than just a decorative scene bathed in blue and gold. 'Streeton has painted a postwar Australian landscape full of national pride, prosperity and potential. The title of the painting further classicises the Australian bush and makes heroes of the colonists who occupied it.' [116] This sense of national pride had its less attractive side: 'If we so choose we can yet be the elect of the world, the last of the pastoralists, the thoroughbred Aryans in all their nobility'. These sentiments were expressed by James MacDonald, then director of the National Art Gallery of New South Wales, writing about Streeton's art in 1931.[117] MacDonald went on to be director at the National Gallery of Victoria. It turns out that Streeton, while active in the protection of the natural environment, held racist views that were at were at the 'extreme end of prejudice'. For example, he responded to the hawkers from the Punjab and Assyria to be seen in Sydney by suggesting that 'an effective way of dealing with the unclean devils would be to shoot them down like dogs wherever they are sufficiently offensive'.[118]

Just to look at, these well-known paintings by Streeton are very easy to love, and for a country full of immigrants they are powerfully Australian, bearing no relation to the landscapes and light of England or Greece or Vietnam. But it is hard to look at them with the same joyful innocence after you have been exposed to a more critical perspective on their content. George Seddon, for example, agrees that the Golden Summers exhibition marks the 'heyday of visual expression of Arcadia' in Australia – the vision of pastoralism in harmony with nature that goes back to Greek mythology. But he goes on to ask where the gold in the paintings comes from – that special quality of light that seemed to gild all it touched. His answer is that it came from the dust in the air, dust from the Western Plains, 'denuded of vegetation, the topsoil pulverised by sheep and cattle and blown to the coast'.[119]

Bill Gammage is just as uncompromising in his response to our favourite representations of rural landscapes. He agrees that Impressionist paintings of 1890s Australia like Streeton's 'declared the colour of Australia'. Earlier depictions of the landscape had relied on a European colour palette of greens, while the Impressionists used 'glaring whites or creams to conjure up the heat and dry of summer'. But they were not painting *Australia Felix*: there are no native grasses in these pictures, as they have already been killed off by over-stocking and erosion, or by deliberate removal:

> Introduced winter or spring flourishing annuals, dead in summer, replaced summer flourishing perennials. *Golden Summer*'s golden creams are colours of death. Conserving drought-shielding perennials took more skill than the newcomers had.[120]

A similar process of critical readjustment is described by George Seddon, who acknowledges how long it took him to become used to the landscapes of Western Australia, and his realisation that he would need to 'learn to see', starting with the plants and especially the wildflowers, which are so easy to like. Landscapes do not present themselves to us as a shared objective reality, but as something shaped by our memories and associations. The same landscape can strike fear into one person and an 'almost cellular affinity' into another.[121] A part of the continent with strong light and little water will have no immediate imaginative resonance for someone who grew up in the damp, fern-covered Dandenongs, or the tropical rainforests of Queensland.

Seddon thinks that the shift in his perception of place was helped by the images being offered to us by particular painters who were explicitly working towards a new sensibility in the wake of the Second World War. As he tells it, he grew acclimatised to Western Australia in the 1950s and 60s while teaching English at UWA, and also completing a science degree, majoring in geology:

> In time I came to find this an absorbing place, full of questions and rewards. I must have acquired a new range of landscape images. Sir Arthur Streeton's hazy landscapes, and others of the Heidelberg School, were supplanted in my mind's eye by the gaunt, clear images of Sidney Nolan.[122]

While Nolan did not paint the Western District, he produced a remarkable series of pictures of the Wimmera in the early 1940s.[123] Later Fred Williams had a similar impact on Australian landscape painting, resisting familiar nationalistic and sentimental portrayals of the bush and gum trees that no longer had much meaning, and presenting us with pictures that are both abstract and yet immediately relevant.

Paintings of our natural environment are important to many of us, which is why galleries return to this theme so often. Some writers think that landscape painting has a particularly significant place in the Australian psyche, because of the relentless and inescapable nature of Australia's geography. A recent national survey of Australians' cultural tastes substantiates this claim, revealing that landscape art is the most popular kind of visual art, though this may not be unique to us.[124] The survey tells us that the three most easily recognised Australian artists are Ken Done, Sidney Nolan and Albert Namatjira, with Namatjira being the most liked of all. The same survey also found that a liking for Aboriginal art transcended the clear division that exists between those who prefer traditional and figurative genres as opposed to those who like contemporary and abstract art. The researchers who conducted the survey suggest a reason for the unusually wide appeal of Aboriginal art: perhaps 'it is something that non-Indigenous Australians felt they ought to like and know more about because of what it has to say about Indigenous culture, its relation to Country, and its significance for Australian culture and identity'.[125]

***

It is not just the native grasses that have disappeared from the landscape. On my friend's pastoral property, not far from the Glenelg River, there are characteristic large paddocks dotted with imposing old river red gums. On several of these trees, standing not far from the homestead, I see the irrefutable evidence of prior occupation in the shape of scars where bark has been cut for a canoe. It had never occurred to me that scarred trees provide a great deal of invaluable information about Aboriginal life before settlement, and that we should protect them as far as possible for this reason.[126] As the settlers took up land in this area conflict ensued, and in the Western District it is estimated that there were at least three massacres in each of which more than thirty Aboriginal people were killed.[127] Richard Broome suggests that between thirty and fifty people died at Fighting Hills near Coleraine in 1840.[128] The Kanalgundidj clan (part of the Jardwadjali language group) are thought to have occupied the area around Casterton prior to white settlement. But by 1857 the clan was already 'nearly extinct'.[129]

The signs that have begun to appear in various parts of Victoria remind us that we are about to enter lands that for thousands of

years have belonged to different clans. There should be more such signs and other marks in the landscape to tell its history, but also memorials to remind us how the continent's human history was ruptured by colonisation and the resistance that occurred. The first time I drove through the area known as the 'Stony Rises', between Colac and Camperdown, I saw it as rough scrubland, closely dotted with low rocky outcrops or hillocks which ran in every direction – a vista of neglect, desolate in winter, in between the large, green, ordered paddocks of surrounding properties. What I did notice, however, was the sudden appearance of kilometres of low, dry-stone walls in place of the usual post and wire fencing – enough to bring on a moment of nostalgia for the Yorkshire Dales. But in reality they seemed an incongruous attempt to tame and frame a landscape that is too big and too raw to be corralled by handmade walls. Otherwise, apart from the walls, the area seemed devoid of interest from the road.

After a few trips through this unwelcoming bit of country, I was given a book called *Designing Place: An Archaeology of the Western District*, in which people from diverse disciplines (such as geology, architecture, history, art and anthropology) show us how they view this landscape. A geologist might well thrill to the fact that 'Eons ago, there were periods when this portion of the Western District was laval porridge puffing up gaseous expulsions and stippling the hot earth's surface with sputtering crater pocks', but even Ross Gibson's vivid prose can't hold my attention for long.[130] I need other ways in.

What did get my attention was reading how Aboriginal resistance fighters would retreat into the Stony Rises, knowing that settlers dare not ride in after them, as the ground presented an impossible terrain for horses. I had known nothing about the prolonged fighting that went on between the arriving British settlers and the traditional owners, the Gunditjmara people, over the first twenty years of settlement around Portland and Port Fairy. The Gunditjmara withdrew into this rocky hiding place, where 'they were occasionally descried by those in pursuit, luxuriating in all the waste of their savage appetite, and flourishing the limbs of their mangled and half-roasted prey'.[131] But this was not like Robin Hood and his merry men retreating into Sherwood Forest to wait out the bad years. Whalers, settlers, station workers and the Native Police Corps, whose assistance was called for by local squatters, were responsible for mass killings of Aboriginal people, including women and children. I am sure someone suggested I read Ralf Boldrewood's *Robbery Under Arms*, when I first arrived in Australia (along with Tom Collins' *Such Is Life* and several other classics that are no longer on anyone's reading list, let alone those of a new citizen). It would have meant little to me in Perth, but now as I criss-cross the Western District it brings the Eumarella War to life, whatever the book's evasions. We are fortunate that 140 years after the publication of *Robbery Under Arms*, Yorta Yorta soprano and composer, Deborah Cheetham has given us her choral and symphonic composition, *Eumarella: A War Requiem for Peace*, in which the story is sung in the dialects of the Gunditjmara people.

By the 1880s the few Aboriginal survivors of this fighting had been removed to the mission on Lake Condah. And to an untutored eye there was little in the broader landscape of the western plains, as I drove across them, that reflected the presence of Aboriginal communities over thousands of years before white settlement. The grassy plains and lightly timbered hills of the 'biggest estate on earth' had long been visually as well as ecologically transformed by those tiny hooves and the industry they created.

***

It is hard to think of anything that has had a more widespread and positive impact on Australians' present-day understanding (and certainly mine) of Aboriginal pre-colonial life than Bruce Pascoe's

Dark Emu. Pascoe set out to make an unassailable case for the widespread practice of agriculture and aquaculture among Aboriginal people across the continent before the arrival of the Europeans, and in so doing to displace popular notions that Aboriginal societies only hunted and gathered wild plants. His sources – the records and diaries of early explorers and colonists – reveal that some first Australians were building dams and wells, farming fish, planting, irrigating and harvesting seeds and then preserving the surplus and storing it in houses, sheds or secure vessels. They were shaping and controlling the landscape to support this way of life, and at the same time relying on the widespread practice of creating and maintaining the famous grassy plains through the use of fire.

In his chapter on aquaculture Pascoe documents the elaborate mechanisms in widespread use across the Western District to trap fish, including the remarkable eel management systems around Lake Bolac, Lake Condah and the Grampians. Here the Gunditjmara people used the local volcanic rock to manipulate water flows, and trap and farm migrating eels and other fish for a reliable food supply, in one of the oldest aquaculture systems in the world. The productivity of these systems allowed villages to be established close by, with stone houses. At Lake Condah for example there are around 200 registered and recorded stone house sites. In 2019 the extraordinary significance of this example of Aboriginal culture was recognised by UNESCO as a World Heritage site, to be known as Budj Bim. Now a partnership between the Gunditj Mirring Traditional Owners Aboriginal Corporation and Melbourne University's School of Engineering is behind a big research project on the engineering processes that enabled the Gunditjmara historically to plan, construct and maintain this aquaculture complex. As part of this a new eel trap was

commissioned from Sandra Aitken, who is the current active Gunditjmara weaver. She learned this skill from her aunt, Connie Hart, whose beautiful baskets are in Museums Victoria and Koorie Heritage Trust collections.[132] The new trap will be prominently displayed in the School of Engineering. With so many tourists travelling the Great Ocean Road to Portland, a stop-off at Budj Bim could do a lot to change the way we all understand what has been lost, and how much it matters that we now have this knowledge.[133]

The sales of *Dark Emu* have been a slow burn by book industry standards, surprising bookseller Mark Rubbo from Readings by becoming his best-selling book for Christmas 2019, five years after its initial publication.[134] Over that year it sold 115 300 copies. In the same year Pascoe produced a version for junior readers, *Young Dark Emu*, which sold out its first print run of 13 000 and won a Children's Book Council of Australia award in 2020. Meanwhile the Aboriginal and Torres Strait Islander dance company, Bangarra, turned this book about agriculture into a successful dance performance, premiering at the Sydney Opera House in 2018. My own – completely untested – theory about its success is that reading how people from a very different culture went about their daily life, in social groupings that can be imaginatively brought to life from these historical records, creates a powerful sense of shared humanity. This shared humanity is, I think, less easily apprehended through an initial focus on belief systems, Indigenous creation stories and the Dreamtime. Everyone can imagine someone else making a fish trap and catching eels, or growing and harvesting yams. It is not so simple to understand why other people believe in skin and clan totems, or re-incarnation or the resurrection, come to that.

Bruce Pascoe's work and his sometimes selective use of secondary sources is coming under strong scrutiny from professional historians and archaeologists, and with luck this will lead to new knowledge and a better understanding of this history. But if this knowledge remains in academic journals then we will all be the poorer. The enthusiasm for Pascoe's book surely reflects a kind of hunger for bridges to be built between Aboriginal history and settler history.

***

Writers like Bill Gammage and Bruce Pascoe have shown a wider public that if you know where and how to look you can see the evidence of 6000 years of agriculture and acquaculture in Victoria's western plains. What is known about this long and varied history depends largely on the work done by the relatively young discipline of archaeology. In his beautifully written account of how archaeologists have transformed our understanding of the evolution of human life in Australia, historian Billy Griffiths reminds us that until the 1960s 'it was widely believed that the first Australians had arrived on this continent only a few thousand years earlier'.[135] By the late 1980s evidence was being collected in Arnhem Land suggesting that people had arrived in Australia perhaps 60 000 years ago – 20 000 years before they arrived in Europe. In 2017 an article in *Nature* confirmed the baseline date for human occupation should now be pushed back to 65 000 years. The extraordinary antiquity of Aboriginal life in Australia made headlines across the world; the New World had become the Old, as Griffiths puts it. It also helped solve the argument between those who believed that all human life came out of Africa and those who believed that *Homo sapiens* evolved simultaneously in different parts of the globe – the multi-regional hypothesis. It seems we all came from Africa, migrating on foot in a single exodus around 70–80 000 years ago.[136]

Reflecting back on the anxieties of this settler nation 'still struggling to come to terms with its deep Indigenous history', Billy Griffiths concludes his book (definitely on my Citizenship reading list) by suggesting that we might connect these parallel stories by placing them within the framework of 'big history' developed by David Christian.[137] By chance, after Proust, I listened to David's extraordinary history of everything as I drove up and down to the Otways and back and forth to Casterton. It takes him eighteen hours talking to get from the Big Bang to the future. I am ready to see the promise in this suggestion.

> Through the lens of big history, the Australian nation quickly becomes a shallow stratum in a richly layered Indigenous place. While such a rendering could be perceived as a threat to the legitimacy of the society that has formed here since 1788, it also holds promise. It is only through the long view of Australian history that we can come to understand the Australian landscape, which is as much cultural as it is natural. It helps us grasp the immensity of human experience on this continent and learn lessons about resilience, adaptability and connections to country. It is a scale that allows us to view ourselves as a species – a vital insight in a warming world. A deep time perspective also presents an opportunity for us to recognise cultures and histories that for so long have gone unrecognised.[138]

The difference between the time scale of Indigenous practices of land management on this continent and those of the pastoral industry is indeed hard to reconcile. The contrast is even greater when you consider how the landscape created from the pastoral industry relates to just a few decades of enormous profitability. The Western District as it exists in the popular imagination is perhaps epitomised by the former prime minister, Malcolm Fraser, with his 9000-acre property, Nareen, near Coleraine. It was 'a pastoral powerhouse, the haven of a social elite and bedrock of its political supremacy for a century and a half'. Richard Zachariah's history of the powerful pastoral families in the area argues that it is now 'just another rural region at the mercy of city-based speculators and international marketeers. The great pastoral dynasties have departed, defeated by economic rationalism and lack of will, disengaged from a land that, if you let it, pushes imagination beyond what one can actually see'.[139] This is undoubtedly an exaggeration as many farmers have managed to adapt and survive, and learned to manage their pastoral properties with infinitely greater environmental care than their predecessors, and I am fortunate enough to visit one of these regularly. Nonetheless, there are major changes occurring in the structure of ownership.

The men who were 'wallowing in wealth' in the 1870s built some grand country houses, many of which still stand, but often far away from any main road and largely invisible to the traveller's eye. Hundreds of homesteads had been constructed by the turn of the century, mostly out of the local hard grey basalt, which Margaret Kiddle thought 'so eloquently expressed the hard Calvinism of the predominantly Scottish pastoralists'.[140] Some settlers adopted the international vocabulary of the Anglo-Indian bungalow, with its broad horizontal spread and wide verandahs, but there were an increasing number of imposing houses in the Picturesque Gothic style. It is hard to love these often daunting bluestone 'manors', which have none of the warm soft colours and texture of the sandstone that dominates Adelaide and Sydney. The National Gallery of Victoria with its beautifully dressed bluestone external walls is one of my favourite buildings, but it is much harder to love the rubble stone walls of Devon Park and Tarndwarncoort, and the period's enthusiasm for 'sombre magnificence'.[141] They make me think of unkind Scottish boarding schools. Barwon Park (1871), which is now owned by the National Trust and open to the public, is a 'stately bluestone pile', covered with striking cast-iron verandahs and balconies across its two-storey front. It was built with the explicit aim of impressing possible royal visitors, but now sits in a sad paddock in a suburban street at the edge of Winchelsea. It seems more notable from today's perspective for its role in the introduction of rabbits to Australia (to give those dignitaries visiting from Britain the amusement of shooting them), than anything else. The sign to the house is pretty well invisible as you drive through Winchelsea. Its existence only came to my attention via a large Princes Highway advertisement for an exhibition of famous wedding dresses one Christmas. Both the house and the exhibition were well worth the entry price. The water closets hidden in the furniture of the main bedrooms were an absolute highlight.

Perhaps my failure to develop any affection for these homesteads is, in part, because those that remain are largely invisible to the public. What my imagination conjures up has been infected by the writer Chloe Hooper's psychological thriller *The Engagement*, in which the well-mannered heir of a pastoral dynasty takes a young Englishwoman for a weekend on the family property, set near the Grampians. 'Warrowill' is a 'grand Victorian mansion seemingly carved out of grey-black volcanic rock', 'swathed in a cast-iron verandah to shelter the ground floor from summer heat'. The woman comes to see that she is being imprisoned, and any escape is unlikely given the sheer distance of the house from the main road: '[A]s far as I could see, there was flat, verdant farmland – no other buildings, just fields, bleak in their sameness, and no sign of those mountains'.[142]

Imagination inevitably comes into play since, as you drive through the Western District today, there is little visible evidence of all the wealth that was created off the sheep's back. Coleraine, with its fine wide main street and evidence of handsome banks, schools, drapers and Masonic hall, now has an IGA and otherwise feels like it could be the set for a nineteenth-century period costume drama. On a couple of occasions I have driven cross-country, avoiding Coleraine, and going through the small town of Merino – the location of Francis and Mary Anne Henty's Merino Downs station. It also has a charming nineteenth-century streetscape, but when I ran out of petrol there on my second passing, I discovered that it is largely uninhabited. This explains why, as you enter the town, you see a large sign announcing, with a fine restrained sense of humour:

> Welcome to
> Merino
> Please slow down
> We don't have
> The people
> To spare

By contrast, Camperdown, in a dairying district, feels like it is still going strong, under the watchful eye of its imposing 100-foot clock-tower, donated to the town by a Manifold, owners of one of the most well-known historic homesteads, 'Purrumbete'. The original property of 100 000 acres was broken up into four to accommodate four sons and subsequently re-sold. The house, cut off from the acreage that paid for it, became a trophy home in the 1980s, traded between such unlikely purchasers as the flamboyant Sydney stockbroker Rene Rivkin and the high-living property developer, originally from Colac, David Marriner.[143]

While you won't see many bluestone manors while driving through the western plains, you will see a surprising number of almost identical wooden bungalows on rural properties, close to the main roads, which look like they have been transported from a modest 1950s

suburb. I guessed that they might be the houses of soldier-settlers built after the Second World War, but so disastrous was the First World War soldier settlement scheme which promised ex-servicemen a future as farmers, that no one seemed to want to know or be able to tell me much about these houses. Around 11 000 Diggers were settled in rural Victoria between 1915 and 1938, but the vast majority were unable to make a living, leaving many of them 'broken both physically and psychologically'.[144] So much has been written about what went wrong with the first scheme – inadequate provision of land and capital, lack of training and falling agricultural prices - that it was hard to find out much about the second scheme, despite the fact that it turns out to be a rather good story. What I am seeing as I drive through western Victoria is the result of an extraordinarily ambitious and carefully designed project which carved out almost 6000 blocks of land across the state as farms for Diggers and their families between 1947 and 1962.[145] Over 3000 of these blocks were compulsorily acquired from some of the large landowners in the Western District, and on each the Soldier Settlement Commission provided a house. The reason they all look the same is because they are indeed all the same, built to rigid specifications, in which the Country Women's Association insisted on proper kitchens. They are generally close to the road because it would otherwise have been too expensive to supply electricity and road access.

The size of the blocks and the selection of soldiers was determined with great care after the disaster of the First World War scheme, and despite the shortage of building materials in the 1950s, a staggering number of houses were built, stimulating the introduction of pre-fabricated construction methods. Victoria settled almost half of the national total of 12 036 soldiers to receive support, and the proportion who failed on their farms was the lowest in the country – a mere 4 per cent. But what is perhaps the most interesting aspect is the national consensus about this being 'the right thing to do' despite its directly redistributive basis. The Rural Reconstruction Commission knew that popular opinion had shifted during the war in support of a 'New Order', offering poorer people opportunities they had not had before. Rather than taking the politically easier route of diverting unused Crown land (generally unused for good reason), the priority was to take farming land, with compensation, from large landowners who appeared not to be making good use of it. Knowledgeable members of the Soldier Settlement Commission spent sixteen years walking around assessing paddocks and land to this end. Any landowner who had lost a son in the war was not approached, but everyone else was fair game, especially absentee landlords.

By the mid-1960s such an influx of population had brought economic growth to many country areas in the Western District, especially small country towns and centres, which now have proper schools, sports facilities and regional libraries.

Reading about this history recently not only helps me make sense of what I see as I drive around the Western District, but resonates with what can be seen as a longer historical narrative about Australia's distinctive political culture, which a visiting Frenchman called 'Le Socialisme sans Doctrines' in 1901.[146] The soldier settlement scheme is of a piece with Australia's distinctive and pragmatic approach to dealing with inequality, in which appealing for a 'fair go' has played a bigger role than class warfare. My interest in the history of the industrial arbitration and the successful integration of so many migrants during this same period makes me perhaps particularly sympathetic to this story.

After the Second World War there was to be one last burst of good fortune for the pastoralists of the Western District, and for the soldier-settlers who chose sheep. This final golden age (more a golden blink of an eye or a golden weekend) was the result of a hardening in the Cold War divisions that emerged from the war. Australia aligned itself with the American-led forces in the Korean War, sending troops in 1950. The war went on for just three years but created intense competition for Australia's wool clip, which was thought to be essential for clothing the Western Alliance's soldiers. The impact of this on the value of wool was immediate and dramatic. The price being paid increased sevenfold during 1951, reaching the record 'pound a pound', a price never seen before. If you had 1000 sheep they went from being worth £2000 to being suddenly worth about £40 000.

Richard Zachariah describes an outbreak of serious extravagance in the middle of the largely austere 1950s, with his father (Headmaster of Hamilton and Western District Boys College) celebrating over a bottle of Scotch with a station owner who had just picked up his annual wool cheque at the Post Office, worth £1 000 000. From his schooldays in Hamilton, Zachariah remembers farmers who went from driving battered utes one week to Rolls Royces the next. 'Some had two Rollers, one for town and the other for the farm.'[147]

Few of those large family properties remain viable businesses today. Many of them have sold off the land that would be necessary for profitable farming, and others cannot afford the upkeep of their historic homes. The farming enterprises that are emerging from the western plains in the twenty-first century are just as hard to understand from the roadside. It is difficult to comprehend the sheer scale of some of the takeover battles occurring in the dairy industry,[148] and the new patterns of land consolidation in the pastoral industry.

Choosing the route through Merino and then cross-country to Port Fairy did, however, take me through a very visible new form of agriculture that sprang up in response to shonky managed investment schemes which funnelled money into blue gum plantations in the 1990s. This fledgling industry imploded under the combined impact of the global financial crisis in 2008 and the tsunami that devastated Japan's paper mills. Many plantings of the eucalypt were ploughed back into the ground as Great Southern Plantations collapsed. Great Southern had raised more than $1.8 billion from 47 000 investors and many of them were seriously burned. Yet ten years later the remaining trees have become valuable again and new plantings can be seen, even on prime pastoral land. At Portland there are 40-metre-high mountains of blue gum woodchips waiting to be shipped out from what locals claim is the single biggest port for the export of hardwood chips in the world.[149] There is no mistaking a blue gum plantation when you drive past one, and they create a landscape that is somehow uglier and more otherworldly than a pine plantation, with no mushrooms to offset the experience. This is perhaps why they rarely front on to major thoroughfares.

I will confess that my understanding of contemporary farming in Australia is idiosyncratic, to say the least. From time to time a copy of something called *AgJournal* appears as an insert in my weekend newspaper. 'Australia's agribusiness magazine' is a boosterish publication launched in 2019 by News Corp, presumably aimed at potential or current investors in Australia's $60 billion agriculture food and fibre industries. This is not a publication in which any downsides to farming practices are going to be discussed, but if you are just interested in the countryside it always has something noteworthy to read.

The inescapable downside is that, to get it, you have to contribute to News Corp's revenue, which I find undesirable, so I may have to give it up. But the August 2020 edition ran a story about the remarkable Chinese investor Qingnan Wen, who now owns what the journalist calls a 'portfolio '(note the investment language) of heritage pastoral properties in western Victoria. These include the Lal Lal Estate (of which I had never heard) south-east of Ballarat, and Mawallock, near Beaufort, which features in Harriet Edquist's photo collection of Western District homesteads and is said to be one of Victoria's grandest and most historic rural properties.[150] I look up Lal Lal and discover it is a 168-year-old property, owned by the Fisken family for six generations, with a century-old Edwardian Arts and Crafts homestead. Mawallock also features a large, handsome Arts and Crafts homestead. I note that both properties have retained the original granite stables built in the 1850s and 1860s. I am tempted to conclude that at some point the family owners decided they did not wish to live in bluestone gothic themselves, but thought the horses would not mind. Mawallock features an important historic garden that could be visited through the Open Gardens Australia scheme in 2019. I missed this but, in any case, I would have been more interested in the off-limits, much admired Arts and Crafts staircase inside the house.

With these purchases Wen now owns 15 000 acres of some of Australia's best grazing and wool-growing country, with the capacity to run more than 60 000 Merino sheep (which of course is nothing compared to the size of earlier pastoral properties). His interest stems directly from his enormously successful textile business near Shanghai, and his ambition is to increase both the quantity and quality of Australian wool supply, at lower prices. For this Wen needs greater scale (more properties will be purchased) and productivity increases through soil improvement and sheep genetics. At Lal Lal, Wen has plans for 'an experimental farm' where industry meetings can bring together 'farmers, wool processors and fashion designers'.[151] I am not sure what images spring to most people's minds when they read about Chinese companies buying up large rural properties, but these kinds of background stories provide a sense of the real people involved in these dramatic changes. I learn that Wen will live at Mawallock, while his grandchildren go to school in Melbourne.

Most Australians probably pass over the *AgJournal* insert in their newspaper just as they pass over the Harvey Norman outer wrapper. But it is one of the few ways to know more about what is happening beyond the vast paddocks you pass as you drive briskly through the countryside to your holiday destination. After ABC Radio National canned its weekly *Bush Telegraph* program at the end of 2014, I became seriously less well-informed about rural life. But now I have (very belatedly) discovered ABC's *Country Hour Victoria* and will be tuning in from time to time. Real farmers tell me that the ABC's rural coverage is no longer connected to real farmers and is instead now aimed at city dwellers.

Even when you read what sounds like a good story it is hard to be in any way romantic about large-scale farming with animals. I found myself on an email list circulating a request that we examine, and then oppose, a planning permit application for a commercial sheep dairy north of Winchelsea. Should this planning permit be successful, just over 14 000 sheep and lambs will be housed and reared 'in confinement' (6000 lactating ewes, 4560 dry and replacement ewes and 3580 reared lambs). This would be the first sheep dairy and confinement facility of its kind in Australia.[152] As an enthusiastic eater of the sheep's cheese made in the French Pyrénées, I have been waiting for Australian cheese makers to get into this. I have toured a farm in Basque country where you follow the sheep out on to the hills and then down into the milking parlour, finishing off with a cheese tasting and opportunity to buy. But to confine – such a euphemism in this context – ewes, whether lactating or not, is a terrible thought, and I would have to boycott whatever cheese or yoghurt came out of there. Those sheep's hooves might not be grinding any grassland to dust, but that would be small comfort.

I lived in Melbourne for decades wrongly imagining that Gippsland was Victoria's dairy country. On my rare trips in that direction I could see cows standing on those green grassy slopes. It was where I had to ask someone what the enormous pale green plastic rolls standing in the paddocks were, since I thought of sileage as something that was kept in a large pit. There was a small dairy farm not far from my place in the Otways but, apart from that, few dairy cows are visible from the main roads. It was only when I started trying out various backroads in the district that I discovered how much dairying was going on. I have now learned that south-west Victoria is the biggest of the eight dairy regions in Australia, increasingly focussed on producing for South-East Asian markets. Not only that, but it is the biggest contributor to the area's economy (30 per cent), generating $4 billion across the whole supply chain.[153]

For someone who likes milk in their coffee, and cheese, I made the mistake of reading an essay in the *Monthly* recently about the life experience of your average Australian dairy cow.[154] It is not good at all. Nor is the health of this important industry more generally. But the author, Lesley Hughes, is primarily interested in explaining why we should want this industry to be a lot smaller than it currently is, so that we can meet carbon reduction goals and also feed the world's population more sustainably. She ends the article with a challenge for her largely urban readers, and one which may well end up as a bigger challenge for Victoria's dairy farmers:

> But what if that two-litre container of white stuff looked like milk, tasted like milk, was chemically identical to milk without the bad bits, was cheaper, made a great cappuccino, came without most of the land, water, climate issues, and nothing had to die to produce it? Would you buy it?[155]

Eating is, as the American writer Wendell Berry said, 'an agricultural act'. Michael Pollan took it further and said that 'eating is a political act'.[156] While the big dairy players may prefer not to see what is coming down the tubes, there are a lot of smaller rural producers all through western Victoria doing things differently and focused on both animal welfare and greenhouse gases. When I see Schulz milk in the supermarket I know where it came from (an organic dairy in Timboon); you can buy pork from free-range heritage breed pigs from Moriac to Eganstown; all over the place you can buy perfectly formed Joe Sgro organic vegetables grown in Yeo, near Colac; nationally recognised sustainable and ethical agro-forestry is practised in Bambra. And these examples are replicated across Victoria (and the rest of Australia). Charles Massy's book about the need to adopt regenerative agricultural practices has slowly seeped into public awareness, with recent discussions on radio and television with national audiences.[157]

It is an idea that has connected six well-established artists, known for their focus on the land, with six regenerative farmers working between the Murray and Murrumbidgee rivers in southern New South Wales. The artists were asked to create art works that expressed their experience of that particular farm, and these have been used to attract the interest of a much wider audience. For example, an exhibition of the works of art is touring regional towns and cities. In 2015 the National Gallery of Victoria (NGV) presented a magical major exhibition of recent works by one of these artists, John Wolseley, who has pushed landscape painting conventions to new limits, 'collaborating' with plants, birds and insects. As Tony Ellwood, director of the NGV, put it, '*Heartlands and Headwaters* presents new possibilities for understanding the Australian landscape in the twenty-first century'.[158]

Perhaps more urgently, economist Ross Garnaut has drawn attention to the ways in which the Australian landscape presents major advantages in capturing carbon:

> The first is our exceptionally large endowment of woodlands, forests and other land relative to population. The second is our exceptional expertise in land-based industries – from agriculture and forestry science, through agricultural and resource economics to public and private knowledge and institutional arrangements supporting commercial success.[159]

The farming landscape of Victoria is changing very fast, but it is not easy to see what is going on and why. As is constantly pointed out, we are an intensely urban nation of immigrants. We start out ill-prepared to understand this continent's geological history, flora and fauna. We cling to the edges of the continent, and definitely need encouragement to get to know the middle better.

Chapter 9
Belonging in an immigrant nation

Immigrants must all wrestle with how they will or can belong in their new country. All sorts of factors will shape how or if they come to feel they belong, including why they came and the way they are welcomed. We only have to contemplate the contrast between the different welcomes offered to British and Chinese immigrants during the gold rushes of the nineteenth century. Historically, immigrants like me, from England, have only ever been regarded with concern – and then with good reason – by Australia's First Nations people. But whether we have been warmly welcomed or given the cold shoulder, we all arrive on a continent that is not immediately intelligible. This is not simply a matter of finding the sun shining at you from the north instead of the south, or Christmas occurring in midsummer (though these things can take a lot of getting used to). We struggle to locate ourselves in these ancient landscapes, dominated by plants and animals that have evolved together, in isolation from the rest of the world, since the great landmass of Gondwana broke apart about 170 million years ago.

Some of the most eloquent and evocative writing about the impact of Australia's geography on our consciousness comes from those who feel entirely at home in the least populated and driest parts of the continent, places that most Australians will never visit themselves. These are not the lush grasslands of *Australia Felix*, but might be the drought-plagued deserts into which Leichhardt and his expedition disappeared while attempting to cross the continent from east to west in the 1840s, never to be found; or the cattle country of far north-western Australia described by Mary Durack in *Kings in Grass Castles*. Tom Griffiths says that Eric Rolls' book, *A Million Wild Acres*, is 'the best environmental history yet written of Australia' and he wants it to be read by 'all Australians'.[160] But it is the story of the Pilliga scrub – 5000 square kilometres of semi-arid woodland in north-central New South Wales. Like thousands of others we drove through it on the Newell Highway heading to Noosa from Melbourne, and did not feel inspired to stop.

For Tim Winton, a writer who describes himself as preoccupied with landscape, it is the semi-arid range country north of Perth where he feels truly at home, where 'the heavens draw you out, like a multidimensional horizon'.[161] In writing about his experiences of landscape, Winton is not merely describing the way his own sensibility has been shaped by growing up on the coast of Western Australia. He goes much further, insisting that the Australian continent impinges on the sensibility of all its inhabitants, in uniquely compelling ways:

> No matter how we live, and what we think of ourselves, the sublimated facts of our physical situation are ever present, and as moving water grinds stones into fresh and often unlikely shapes, the land presses in, forever wearing, pushing, honing. Most of the time we barely register the attrition. In a disembodied era of digital technology and franchise culture there are periods when even an Australian at home can feel he or she might be anyplace, or perhaps no place at all. But wildness soon intervenes to disabuse us. The pressure of geography reasserts itself palpably and unmistakably to remind us that, of course, we could only be *here*.[162]

The pressure of geography is felt in most places, and this recognition of place would, I think, be as strong in the Lake District as on the edge of the Nullarbor. But this passage resonates because I think our geography wears and pushes more than most, though perhaps this is an immigrant's response. Reading Winton's account of the way he reacted to the light and landscapes of Europe was instantly recognisable to me as the mirror image of my own reactions to the light and landscapes of Western Australia when I arrived from England. Finding himself living in Europe in the 1980s, Winton is surprised by his 'inability to connect bodily and emotionally' to this new environment. His largely Eurocentric education prepared him to feel very much at ease, yet what he experienced instead was a pervasive sense of unease. Travelling in the opposite direction to him, and landing first in Perth, I also experienced a pervasive sense of unease.

My flight via Bombay reached the northern Australian coastline in daylight on a February afternoon, and then turned southward, following the west coast until it landed at the airport, on the northern edge of the city. As I sat, staring out of my porthole in the sky, I saw no sign of human habitation, just an ocean of what looked like sand stretching away to the east. For some time afterwards I remained unnerved by the sheer volume of uninhabited land around me. Winton, on the other hand, was unsettled by the vistas of 'almost unrelieved enclosure and domestication' he met in Europe. (Robert Macfarlane, the English writer about the natural world, had not yet published his book on finding *The Wild Places* which remain in Britain and Ireland.) Even in the mighty Alps he found no escape from the evidence of human intervention; 'around every mountain pass and bend it seems there is another tunnel, a funicular, a fashionable resort or a rash of reflective signage'. While I found the light in Perth blinding and unrelenting, making me long for clouds, Winton thought bright days in Europe might be 'pretty in a painterly sort of way' but they 'lacked the white-hot charge my body and spirit yearned for'. Mind you, another Australian writer said pretty much the same thing back in 1905 at the age of twenty-three, when she too found herself in England missing home, and her poem found a huge audience. Everyone knows the second verse, 'I love a sunburnt country, A land of sweeping plains, Of ragged mountain ranges, Of drought and flooding rains'. But Dorothea McKellar's first verse is about not being able to share the love English people have for 'green and shaded lanes', 'brown streams and soft, dim skies'. There is nothing soppy about her image of home:

> Core of my heart, my country!
> Her pitiless blue sky,
> When sick at heart, around us
> We see the cattle die –

The loss of the place that shaped your imagination in early life is of course common to the experience of migration, but is it particularly difficult for immigrants to feel at ease in the Australian landscape? And is it necessary to feel at home in the landscape in order to feel Australian?

Winton's view is that even after two centuries of European settlement, 'Australia is still a place where there is more landscape than culture', where there is 'for every built structure a landform twice as large and twenty times more complex. And over it all, an impossibly open sky, dwarfing everything'. The land, he believes, will eventually 'make people anew', but this does not happen quickly. 'Many of us are startled to learn how different we are from our immigrant and convict forebears, for this is a place that eventually renders people strangers to their origins.'[163]

Kim Mahood, a writer and artist, who grew up near the Tanami Desert in northern Australia, on her family's cattle station, Mongrel Downs (how Australian is that?), agrees that 'geography shapes who we are and how we think'.[164] For Mahood, leaving this landscape to live and work near Canberra involves loss. Her two volumes of memoirs are both shaped around returning to the country between the Tanami Desert and the East Kimberley, where she feels 'alive with an intensity I feel nowhere else'.[165] Heading out from Alice Springs towards Mount Isa, she is already moving into these overwhelming landscapes. 'It is the kind of country which would take hold of you if you stayed in it for long. In the winter it is riven by bitter winds, and in summer can become a monochrome wasteland. Unrelenting places seem to brand the psyche as gentle green places never can'.[166] The intensity of this response to the landscape reminds me of Jill Ker Conway's lyrical description of the western plains of New South Wales where 'the earth meets the sky in a sharp black line so regular that it seems as though drawn by a creator interested more in geometry than the hills and valleys of the Old Testament. Human purposes are dwarfed by such a blank horizon'.[167]

While Mahood's memoirs describe a deeply personal and life-long exploration of her relationship with this remote part of the continent and both its Aboriginal and settler inhabitants, she observes the country and its people without sentiment. She writes with extraordinary tenderness about the vulnerability of the white men 'scattered all through the country whose lives seemed forever on the verge of being overtaken by fate'. They were constantly injuring themselves, 'bits of windmills fell on them, horses kicked them, bad food and too much rum poisoned them, minor extremities were torn off by ropes and machinery'. They had pregnant girlfriends, got into brawls without thinking. 'Their lives ran along an edge that threatened to cut them to pieces.' The men she knew came north looking for 'a place where the constraints of society were more elastic'.[168] Mahood is drawn to the real lives of these men 'that lent validity to the Outback myth with which I identified'. At the same time she is sceptical about the 'whitefellow' myth of solitude, which is 'about finding some sort of redemption in the solitary encounter in a spiritual domain, which is epitomised by the desert'.[169]

Reading descriptions of the country that has shaped the identities of these Australian writers does not make me want to visit that country, but they do exert some kind of significant imaginative influence on me. And I am intrigued by Mahood's uncertainty about why the continent exerts such a spell:

> Many people, including those who are not Australian, are powerfully struck by the ancestral nature of the Australian landscape. I wonder if it is because the country has been held in the consciousness of its people in this particular way, this extraordinary identification of people with country so that the two are not distinguishable from each other. Or is it in the nature of certain places to assert a grip on the imagination of all who set foot in it, and to draw out of them whatever they have to offer?[170]

The experience of those who migrate to Australia as adults and find themselves living in these powerful Australian rural landscapes is less well documented. Perhaps this is why, on my only proper visit to the National Museum of Australia in Canberra, the exhibit that captured my attention most directly was the Diana Boyer collection. It records the imaginative and emotional response of one immigrant woman who settled on a farm in rural New South Wales in the early 1980s, after she and her husband fled political violence and repression in their home country, Argentina. For almost three decades Boyer, a trained botanical illustrator, painted, took photographs and documented her surroundings.[171] I identify immediately with her when she says: 'When you move you have to find something that is meaningful to you and that in some ways will help you come to terms with where you are. Although Binalong is a very beautiful little place, I think I needed to understand why I was there'.[172] Moving degrees of longitude but not latitude, and without urban anchors, Boyer's perspective is different to mine.

> Perhaps it is not so important if one migrates from city to city but in the country, the sky becomes the point of reference. I was relieved to find the Southern Cross here as well.

As the sun was setting over her property to the west, Boyer could talk on the phone to her mother in Argentina as that same sun was coming up.

***

There is no doubt that Australia's vast and thinly populated land has stimulated some compelling landscape writing – writing that illuminates the way the continent's most distinctive geographical characteristics have shaped sensibility and identity. But can anyone claim to speak for the people of the whole continent? When Tim Winton writes that the 'pressure of geography reasserts itself palpably and unmistakably to remind us that, of course, we could only be *here*',[173] where is 'here'? It could be argued that his sensibility is distinctively local, and that much of what he describes as his 'home' would not be recognisable to Victorians or Tasmanians, or even Queenslanders from the wet tropics. It could, nevertheless, be argued that even in our cities, geography makes itself felt in peculiarly Australian ways.

In Melbourne the sky is often a strong blue of the kind that you would never see in England, but such a colour might be quite familiar if you come from southern Italy or Greece; and there is almost always a cloud waiting to scud across the sky. But Melbourne is perhaps always the exception. George Seddon, writing about garden design, wants us to recognise that in Australia 'the natural environment – the bush – is still a powerful physical presence in all the capital cities', but he too admits Melbourne may be different.[174] Like me, he thinks it is quite easy to pretend you are not in Australia if you are in Melbourne. Even as you move away from the city itself you are confronted with suburbia for 35 kilometres as you travel east, and a landscape dominated by new suburbs and flat paddocks to the west. This is a long way from any experience that could be compared to 'standing on a saltpan the size of a small country'.[175]

From Tasmania Henry Reynolds explicitly rejects the possibility of feeling at home in 'Australia'. Despite living and working for most of his adult life in Queensland he only belongs in Tasmania. Returning in retirement, he says that 'never has the island been more important to him than now. In Hobart he feels closer to his deceased parents'. Interviewed by the historian Peter Read, Reynolds says that: '*I can sense them because I've walked with them there.*' Importantly, his sense of belonging is both physical and social, involving 'the light, the shadows and the sky, the way the sun is in the sky ... One day I realised the sun was where it should be, where it really belonged ... There's something about the southern latitudes and the wind and the sky and the light, day and night which is quite distinctive'.[176]

For Tom Griffiths it is not empty panoramas or light that feeds his awareness of being Australian but transformed and humanised landscapes. In particular, the central Victorian goldfields where his ancestors settled in the 1850s speak to him. This is a worked-over landscape, with 'eroded gullies, the unexpected depressions, the mullock heaps, the old mine chimneys, the messy buildings of the functional towns'. Just as Don Watson wants us to see the bush for what it really is and what we have done to it, Griffiths identifies with the 'consciousness of human presence, beneficial or harmful, the ephemerality of much European settlement, the successive advance and retreat of generations, each leaving its imprint on the landscape'.[177]

Despite all these qualifications I am inclined to think that Tim Winton is still right when he says that, wherever you are on this continent, there is something relentless about the Australian place itself, and that this explains why Australian writers and painters continue to fixate on landscape. 'We are a place where the material facts of life must still be contended with.'[178] Whatever my localist or particularist quibbles about his claims, he is describing his own Australian-ness in ways that resonate with me. I can, after several decades, identify with his words, and they reassure me that it is no personal failing of mine that I have had to struggle to feel at home in the country – despite my ease in the social and political environment.

***

While Australia's physical geography does not make it easy for a European immigrant to feel at home, its social geography is also discomforting, mapping a nation founded on the dispossession of its first inhabitants – inhabitants who had been here for at least 60 000 years before Governor Arthur Phillip laid claim to New South Wales and before the Henty family started to invade the Western District with sheep. These maps, physical and social, are sometimes seen as dividing the continent in two. Kim Mahood tells us about her love of driving through South Australia, up the Stuart Highway, 'a form of space travel, a reminder of the scale and existential strangeness of this country'. On her long drives through this particular landscape she is able to revisit what she calls a cultural disjunction within Australia, a gap that is both geographic and psychological:

> Retaining an embodied sense of this is central to what I do, since the gap between the urban, Eurocentric, aspirational, heavily populated south-east corner of the continent and the remote, predominately Aboriginal, barely sustainable, thinly populated pocket of desert is the space in which my writing and my art practice are made.[179]

Through this second memoir Mahood engages in an on-and-off dialogue with a long-standing artist friend, Pam, who has come to the view that white and Indigenous ways of occupying the land are incompatible. For her friend, this means always 'feeling out of place'.[180] Others may be less adamant than Pam, but still disconcerted. Saskia Beudel is another writer who has published a memoir in which the Australian landscape plays an implacable role. She describes how, while holidaying as a child with her family near Wilsons Promontory, a farmer showed her the spot where Aboriginal people, not so long ago, had sat eating shellfish looking out over the sea. She became aware of an historical landscape, and 'first sensed an absence in my surroundings that is the tone of a colonised land'.[181] In her book, *A Country in Mind: Memoir with Landscape*, she identifies particular difficulties that arise when you write 'from a settler culture such as Australia's, where the question of dispossession is still pressing and unsettling'.[182]

The Aboriginal land rights movement that began in the 1960s, and the legal recognition of Aboriginal claims to land title that have flowed from its success, have made it impossible to ignore the colonial past, even if you live in the increasingly cosmopolitan south-east corner of the continent. At demonstrations across the continent demanding an end to discrimination, it is common to see signs insisting that Australia 'Always was, always will be Aboriginal land'. Midnight Oil told us not only that they were 'Sorry', but also insisted in 'Beds are Burning' that we should 'pay the rent'. This visible contestation over shared country and claims to 'home' have created both unease and celebration. At one end of the spectrum we have seen Germaine

Greer loudly announce that she will never return to live in Australia unless a treaty is signed with the Aboriginal people, while Judith Wright has written about her conflicted conclusion, that 'the two strands – the love of the land we have invaded, and the guilt of the invasion – have become part of me'.[183] At the other end of the spectrum many more recent immigrants see no connection between their pasts and the historic acts of dispossession, looking to belong in what they see as an intrinsically multi-cultural society.

If you want to know what 'Australians of every variety' feel about how they belong to a divided country at the end of the twentieth century, and how they place themselves 'in relation to the Indigenous past and present', then a good place to start is Peter Read's book *Belonging: Australians, Place and Aboriginal Ownership*. Read has talked to 'young Australians, Asian Australians, foreign-born Australians, rich Australians, seventh-generation Australians, rural Australians, just-arrived Australians, poets, artists, country and western musicians, atheists, metaphysicians, spiritualists, those who have worked closely with Aboriginals, those whose land is under Indigenous claim, those who have yet to meet an Indigenous person face to face'. [184] You are almost bound to find someone in these pages with whom to agree, or who crystallises a feeling for you, or someone with whom to disagree. For myself, I wanted to continue the discussion with the four women speaking to Peter Read in the chapter called 'Women's Business', and the four historians in the chapter that follows, each of whose professional work has been devoted to Indigenous or environmental history.

The two most well-known historians researching the Aboriginal people of Tasmania could not have more divergent views about their sense of belonging. Lyndall Ryan loves the land with a passion, but feels she 'can never belong'. She 'sensed that land had a much deeper significance for Aboriginal people than it could ever have for others', and that 'we have to really recognise that it's Aboriginal country'. No matter her unusual and longstanding closeness to particular Aboriginal communities, she cannot escape her destiny because 'we must remain forever the descendants of the invaders'.[185] The contrast with Henry Reynolds could not be any sharper as he tells us that he is 'unable to share the view of those who feel they don't really belong in Australia, that they are barely tolerated guests or that they will always be alienated from the land'.[186] Here, again, is the contrast in sentiments expressed by Kim Mahood and her friend, who represents what Mahood sees as the 'intellectual and academic temper' of her time, shaped by a sense of post-colonial guilt. Indeed, Mahood's map of social division cuts quite differently. She knew white people 'who felt for the country as deep an emotional and physiological attachment as the traditional custodians, and were more like them in their social and psychological temper than they were like urban Australians of any race'.[187] I have met farmers who feel a similar gulf between their own attachment to the land and the attitudes of even well-meaning city dwellers. It is the same kind of sentiment that provoked journalist Gabrielle Chan to write *Rusted Off: Why Country Australia Is Fed Up*.

The sheer diversity of people who speak in Read's book challenges any simple notion of the 'we' and 'us' in Australia. Australia has an undeniable colonial past, but it is also one of the world's major 'immigration nations' (together with New Zealand, Canada and the US). Today, almost 30 per cent of the population was born overseas, and while for a long time most of us came from the original colonial power, this is no longer the case. In 2010 the highest numbers of permanent immigrants came from China and India. (New Zealand citizens also feature highly in the number of settler arrivals, but they are not counted under Australia's Migration Program unless they apply for, and are granted, a permanent visa.) One of the four women speaking to Peter Read in the 'Women's Business' chapter is Marivic Wyndham, who left Cuba as a girl after Castro seized power, moved to the US, and while there married an Australian diplomat, arriving in Australia around the same time I did in the mid-1970s. Another of the four women, Manik Datur, grew up in Calcutta, moving to live in London as a teenager, before the family migrated to Melbourne. Both these women have made personal connections with Aboriginal communities, Marivic through a particular friendship and Manik through working in Alice Springs for the Central Land Council.

For these women their sense of belonging is rooted in social relations, not geography or history. Marivic says she 'belongs to Australia because she can take part in its conversation and because she believes in its virtues', though at the same time she sometimes rages that the Anglo-Celtic Australians might 'spit her out'.[188] She sees Australia as 'multi-centred', and that Aboriginality is one of those centres. After a return visit to Cuba in the 1990s she came to see that 'Australia is home', even though she did not lose the sense that her people are Cubans.[189]

For Manik the idea and reality of a cultural mix is nothing new, growing up in India with its long history of invasion by Greeks, Persians and Moghuls before the British. She belongs in Australia 'because she has consciously grafted herself here; because she likes the look of the land; because it gives her space as a non-Anglo-Celtic Australian; because she feels accepted by its people; because she holds a commitment to its democracy; because of her memories and because occasionally ... she feels an ache for the land' from her Canberra suburb.[190] Like Marivic, she knows that Australia must be multi-centred so that everyone can belong, and thinks that it is a mistake to place too much emphasis on memories of place. The key to belonging, for her, is social connectedness.

It is not unreasonable to think of Australia as a young society, where not too much is set in concrete, and where there is space and time for these different kinds of belonging to acknowledge each other and create space for each other. But even though recent immigrants may recognise that Aboriginal voices must be heard, this in itself does not address the particular damage done by colonial dispossession. The Uluru Statement from the Heart seems like an extraordinary moment in the evolution of relations between Aboriginal communities and the settlers, but for that reason its out-of-hand rejection by Prime Minister Malcolm Turnbull felt, to me, like a slap in the face to all of us. Marivic may not have been disheartened, however, since in her view 'the right of reconciliation has been taken away from the people, it only occurs politically, not face to face, and it's set up along adversarial lines'. Instead, she would like her personal relationship with her Aboriginal friends to be 'repeated ten million times'.

Reading individual accounts of belonging inevitably sparks moments of personal recognition or its opposite, or a sense of comfort or discomfort. If you read too many the effect is slightly numbing as individual differences overwhelm any sense of shared social or political frameworks. Everyone is just different. This was how I felt after reading too many of the 27 short stories of migration pulled together in the cleverly titled volume, *Joyful Strains: Making Australia Home*. The editors are both writers who moved here from the USA, but their contributors are as varied in their backgrounds as Peter Read's. As my attention began to wander the 14th chapter suddenly produced an integrative framework that instantly had me taking notes. Ghassan Hage is a well known anthropologist and social theorist who has written widely on multiculturalism, white nationalism, and colonialism.

But he is also an immigrant who grew up in Beirut – albeit with Lebanese grandparents who had settled in Bathurst in the late 1930s – who was sent to Sydney as a young man to escape the violence in Lebanon. In his chapter he describes visiting the house his grandparents had lived in, while en route with his family to a party in Cowra. Standing in the garden looking at the fruit trees planted by his grandfather more than 50 years earlier, he is overwhelmed by a sudden sense of feeling 'rooted *here*, feeling more Australian than ever.'[191]

Curious about this unexpected reaction, he acknowledges that his hard-wired, proud, 'politically correct' awareness of Australia's colonial history with its violence, domination and appropriation, 'did not diminish the sense of rootedness they [his grandfather's trees] infused in me'. Here the social theorist comes into play, offering him the idea of a 'rootedness' that was not 'possessive', that did not and could never claim 'monopoly over the space of its emergence'.

> For many people, a greater sense of rootedness does not mean a sense of being locked in the ground, unable to move. On the contrary, roots often are paradoxically experienced like an extra pair of wings. And this was exactly how I experienced my trees. I felt them propelling me.

The roots Ghassan is talking about do not keep you grounded, but stay with you as you move – so his connection to his grandfather's trees is propelling him forward not holding him back. He glimpses a 'mode of belonging that can stand in opposition to the narrow territorial way of being rooted…which has often generated sadness and paranoia'. This territorial way of being rooted belongs to a kind of 'exclusivist mentality, which operates with an either/or logic: either my roots or yours; either this land is yours or mine; either you belong here or there; either you are sovereign or I am.' But what Ghassan experienced is a quite different kind of rootedness.

> It is not an anti-colonial belonging, which pits the belonging of the colonised against that of the coloniser while conserving colonialism's either/or logic. Nor is it a post-colonialism, which prematurely sees colonial culture as something superceded.

What is being experienced, not just theoretically, is a space beyond the colonial culture, 'showing us that another mode of belonging is possible'.[192]

Chapter 10
Where I am

I bought a place in the country because the country was where I knew I did not feel at home, even after thirty-five years of living in Australia. I now understand a lot more about why many English immigrants might find it hard to feel at home outside our major cities and towns, but I found this out more by reading than by gardening or minding my cows. In fact, if I had read enough beforehand about the way Australian landscapes shape identity and feelings of belonging, then I might have concluded that I should head into the Little Desert in western Victoria, or better still the Gibson Desert in Western Australia, rather than cosying down in the Otways. I did eagerly buy Nicholas Rothwell's *Wings of the Kite-Hawk* when it came out in 2003, in which he sets out to retrace the routes taken by the great nineteenth-century explorers of inland Australia, reliving their largely unhappy experiences. Fortunately, I did not find it a compelling read. Once is enough to hear the story of Captain Sturt and his party, carrying a small boat all the way into the centre of the continent only to find 'tall sand-dunes, in numberless succession, receding one after another as far as the eye could see, the peak of each ridge flame-red, above deep, shaded blurs of sickly purple vegetation. They had come upon a sand-wave desert; a frozen sea'.[193]

These vast, thinly populated and dry expanses of country feature strongly in our collective imagination, appearing in so much Australian writing and film making, yet the result is often to render them less approachable and more unknown. The historian Mark McKenna bought eight acres of land on the far south coast of New South Wales in the early 1990s, as a bush retreat. While he was looking for the land, estate agents expressed surprise that he would want something inland from the coast. As he wrote in his history of this small corner of the continent, 'for many people in the area, the distance from the coast to the hinterland is not measured in kilometres: it is imagined, a psychological frontier beyond which civilisation is left behind'. 'Everywhere today in the small communities throughout Eden-Monaro, there is a feeling of being detached from the imaginary heartland of the state – one that is liberating but also leaves many feeling vulnerable.' [194]

Looking at it now, it is hard to see how gardening and minding some cows in the Otways was going to help my own imaginative possession of this continent. But if you enjoy gardening, as so many Australians do, then I think making a garden can – like reading – change your feelings about belonging or not belonging to the land. I am tempted to say that we *should* change our relationship to the land, but no-one chooses a garden style out of a sense of moral obligation – apart perhaps from the permaculture disciples. We learn to garden mostly by doing, by remembering our childhood experiences, and from our attempts to re-create something familiar and pleasurable. It is a tiny minority who see gardening as an opportunity to experiment. Immigrants may, in fact, understandably try to avoid noticing that they are gardening in radically different environments to those they come from. I now live in an inner-ring suburb of Melbourne that

has been dominated by Greek immigrants for the past seventy years. Every second house in the nearby streets where I walk my dog has at least one olive tree either in its front garden or in the nature strip, and a lemon and an orange tree if there is space, together with a few tortured standard roses. I acknowledge that it could be argued that Greek choices make better sense than English ones, as the olive is a tree with narrow grey-green leaves designed to withstand sun and heat – the iconic tree of the Mediterranean. It is also a tree which comforts European immigrants by speaking to our cultural values, reminding us of the Bible, or Ancient Greece.

But I am with George Seddon when he insists that 'Mediterranean' is not a useful concept in Australian gardening, given the latitude of our cities; we need to think Morocco not south of France. The challenge he presents to us, however, is not merely horticultural:

> We share these cultural values, they are equally a part of the background of many of us, but [the olive tree] is not iconic of Australia. It might be time to redirect our dreams. We are here, and not somewhere else. There are design and planting alternatives.[195]

I confess I have not tried discussing this idea with my Greek neighbour, as I hand over some of my tomato seedlings or return her feijoas which fall on our side of the fence. It is a brave person who tells another gardener that they are out of line. Perhaps there are other small steps to gardening change, like learning about the fragility of the continent's soils and the unreliable rainfall, or discovering the unique flora that have evolved here, and which are increasingly available in all nurseries. A bigger step might involve re-thinking the kinds of feelings or sentiments that you wish your garden to induce.

I say all this tentatively because – I will confess straight out – my country garden-making was a failure on as many fronts as it was a success. In particular, I failed to make a garden that was significantly different from one I might have made in England. In my defence, I could argue that it took me far too long to take out all the exotic planting that I inherited. It was difficult to destroy so many well-established plants that were hard-wired into my gardening vocabulary. My gardening notes indicate that in the end I paid the local tree remover to take out well over forty trees, and I slowly dug out as many large shrubs. But as I cleared away everything that was in the

wrong place, so I created spots where I could not resist finally being able to plant things that I had never in my life had space for – like the aptly named wedding cake bush, *Viburnum plicatum mariesii*, and a pair of my favourite crab apples on either side of the stone steps which I had built for me from local granite, leading from one terrace to the next.

I would have been happy to begin this project from an empty paddock, but that is not what presented itself. Or when it did, I lacked the courage to start from scratch in a tin shed. From time to time I did confront the fact that I had no coherent master plan (the *sine qua non* of good garden design, according to my favourite books). But small victories over one or other corner of the garden helped to put off the final realisation that, after five years, gardening had not – in itself – helped me to feel at home in this Victorian landscape. I did finally define one side of the garden, where there were some pleasing eucalypts and casuarinas planted as a windbreak along the fence line, as a native plant area – an area which began to give me great pleasure as I experimented with grevilleas and poas, spyridium and Big Red kangaroo paws. But if I am honest, it was a token effort.

Something profound had, nonetheless, shifted in my gardening subconscious. In 2015, while visiting my Parsee friend in London, I found she had organised tickets for us to go to the Chelsea Flower Show. After twenty years of long-distance membership of the Royal Horticultural Society (RHS), I was finally undertaking my version of the Hajj, visiting Mecca. Until I went, I hadn't realised I was no longer a believer. While there were one or two really admirable and interesting show gardens to explore, I discovered that I felt no nostalgic pangs and certainly no need ever to go again. For me, the most memorable element of the show was the enormous carpet of knitted red poppies commemorating the centenary of the First World War, laid out over the lawns in front of the Chelsea barracks, a project started by two Australian women. Last year I did not renew my subscription to the RHS journal, and this year I have gone so far as to un-follow nearly all the English gardens and gardeners I most admire on Instagram. I honestly don't think I would care if I never saw another long perennial border, not because they are not beautiful, but because they no longer speak to me personally. Given that it has taken me forty years to get to this point, humility suggests I should be patient with my friends who still plant camellias.

So, buying some land did not, sadly, turn me into Fiona Brockhoff. I bit off more than I could chew. But my gardening failures should not detract from my success in making myself at home in the country, from the simple pleasures of echidna watching and yabby catching, to worrying about the future of agriculture in Australia. I may have failed Eucalypt Identification 101, but I am most definitely now at home among the gum trees, and will not be surprised to see a tiger snake up the top of one. I understand the way they burn and why birds fight over them. I have experienced pure happiness watching the low, late rays of summer sun lighting up the strip of tall manna gums along my southern fence-line, or the low, early-morning rays of sun coming across the paddock from the dam to the cow-trimmed fringes of the casuarina trees in the shelter belt.

I sincerely believe that if I were to start again today I would make a garden that looks and feels very different. I have now seen enough beautiful plantings that are of this place and for this place that my sensibility has been permanently transformed. But I also realise that there is a large element of unrealistic thinking in 'what I would do if I could start again', since I am now channelling Patrice Newell, the Sydney TV presenter turned biodynamic farmer, with her 10 000 acres in the Hunter Valley.[196]

***

It has been suggested that after the First World War particular images of the Australian landscape were promoted as popular and widely shared symbols of the young nation's identity, promising social, economic and political stability. The pastoral ideal also manifested itself in quite concrete ways, such as the returned soldier settlement scheme, for which 24 million acres had been set aside by the mid-1920s. The terrible lessons learned from the abject failure of that scheme are the inspiring backdrop to the Second World War scheme that shaped so much of rural Victoria in particular. Yet it is hard to imagine anyone today proposing that Australian identity rests on such pastoral ideals, despite our enthusiasm for annual Agricultural Show days – though perhaps liking to be outdoors, camping and playing sport might be their modern-day descendants? If the pastoral ideal has lost its purchase on our imaginations, do our imaginations still suggest that in order to feel at home in Australia we need to feel at home in its landscapes?

In working my way around this question I discover how often the final paragraph from Bill Gammage's book is quoted by reviewers and other writers. It is an eloquent appeal to our better natures, and an exhortation. 'We have a whole continent to learn. If we are to survive, let alone feel at home, we must begin to understand our country. If we succeed, one day we might become Australians.'[197] A similar sentiment surfaces in Tim Winton's writing when he urges us to see Australia as a physical entity, much more than as a political idea or an economy, pressing us to acknowledge that where we are defines who we are. Like Bill Gammage, he wants us to redefine our sense of collective identity, arguing that concepts of patriotism have evolved so far that they no longer require devotion to an 'abstraction like the state'. Instead the focus of a 'true patriot' will be the 'the web of ecosystems that make a society possible', as if 'the land were kith and kin'.[198]

It is not difficult to understand the emotions behind this kind of appeal, and the more so as the warming climate begins to threaten these 'ecosystems' in visible and distressing ways. Over the summer of 2019–20, terrifying bushfires burned 97 000 square kilometres of Australian land. Scientists have estimated that 1 billion animals died in these fires, adding another forty-nine species to the already long endangered list.[199] Our capacity to absorb the significance of these facts is, I think, much less than our capacity to empathise with the humans who experienced the fires directly. We are in clear need of help in making sense of what is happening.

There is something about the demands of last sentences, with which to complete important pieces of writing, that often seems to lead to portentousness, or over-simplification at least. Even George Seddon's normally dry and often acerbic tone deserts him in the last paragraph to his final book, *The Old Country*, published in 2005. He acknowledges post-colonial Australia is a multicultural society, 'rich in many ways', but rightly notes that 'its adaptation to the physical realities of an old unyielding land is not one of them'. He closes the book by asserting that 'Being Australian in the sense of belonging to the land has always depended on an acquired skill. It is neither a right nor a given; it has always had to be learnt, once handed down by the tribal elders to the young, then earned by them ... It has always been a title to be earned, and so it remains'.[200]

There are, I think, several problems with this privileging of landscape and country in concepts of belonging in Australia, even if Seddon does perhaps allow that there are other potential ways to 'be Australian'. The first problem is the inconvenient fact that so many Australians feel they belong to this country without any particular affinity for its lands. Even Mark McKenna, who writes so clearly about how living in the bush has 'deepened and sharpened his attachment to the land', makes it clear at the beginning of his book that he is 'not one who believes "the land" is the only source of spiritual belonging in Australia'.[201] Like many of us who have made our way in a global network of professional and family connections, McKenna can feel he belongs in Sydney, or London, as well as the south coast of New South Wales, even if for different reasons.

Some would go even further and say that the key to their belonging in Australia has nothing to do with the land or its landscapes. Marivic and Manik tell Peter Read that they belong to a society, not a place. Marivic, from her Cuban origins, insists that her sense of belonging has 'not much to do with gum trees, light or space', but rests on her sense of Australia as a 'decent society' – a society which people who have not seen 'the horrors of the rest of the world' fail properly to appreciate. To this strong sense of civic commitment, she adds that her sense of belonging is distinctively female, because giving birth to a child here is a powerful claim on a bit of this earth 'not because she protected it in battle but because here was where her body met this place'.[202] Manik, born in Calcutta, has a less bodily and more cerebral attachment to Australia, suggesting that you can belong 'by intellectual engagement, through affinity, through one's acceptance by the place, by the local people; and one can belong through contribution to the place'.

No one could suggest that Peter Read avoids any inconvenient facts in his quest to understand how Australians, in all their contemporary diversity, feel they belong, and this steers him to less portentous and more prosaic conclusions. His methodology perhaps inevitably leads him to say that 'Belonging is ultimately personal'. 'We can belong in the landscape, on the landscape, or irrelevantly to the landscape. We don't all have to belong to each other. To understand that is a step to belonging.'[203] But there is a sharp point to this seemingly anodyne conclusion, stemming from Read's decades of research into Aboriginal history. 'Belonging-in-parallel does not imply that the majority cultures pretend that the Aboriginals don't exist.' For Read, 'belonging means sharing and that sharing demands equal partnership'.[204]

***

So where do I find myself coming to rest in all this discussion about belonging? It will be obvious that, for me, landscape matters. I have found it hard to feel fully at home in landscapes that I don't understand and which neither contain nor reflect any of the elements that shaped my sensibility as a child. Many Australian-born people have written about their feeling of intense connection to one or other particular landscape or place on this continent, and indeed it would be implausible to profess love for every bit of it, from the Tanami Desert to Tasmania's Franklin River. The battle to save the Franklin River from the planned hydroelectric dam was won through a High Court decision in 1983, the culmination of the biggest environmental struggle in Australian history. Frank Bongiorno suggests that the battle for the Franklin 'signalled for white Australians a new way of relating to place, a love of country that amounted to something more complex – and more attractive – than classical nationalism's appeal to "blood and soil".[205] Billy Griffiths reminds us that the judgement that saved the river was not based on the need to preserve a 'wilderness', an 'ancient pure, timeless landscape'. It was the archaeological research that was undertaken 'in the heat of the campaign' and which revealed that 'far from being untouched and pristine, southwest Tasmania had a deep human history. What was undoubtedly a natural wonder was also a cultural landscape'.[206]

Winton is not asking us all to love his bit of the continent, but 'to revere the web of ecosystems that make a society possible', and to be ready to defend them passionately. His language is discomforting to me, but I am not sure exactly why since I understand and sympathise with its purpose. Is there a masculinist eco-warrior lurking here? It seems to lack the wisdom to be found in Kim Mahood's description of her own, intense love of the Tanami Desert. She knows it is 'an unrequited love story, because it is between a person and a place, and a place doesn't love you back'. Or perhaps, she thinks, 'it's like loving God, and what you get back is a reflection of what you put in'.[207]

I don't think that Winton's exhortations that we become real patriots – passionate defenders of our eco-systems – are likely to motivate anyone not already committed to the cause. On reflection I found myself more troubled by his casual dismissal of old-fashioned patriotism towards 'an abstraction like the state'. I was reminded of Michael Ignatieff's book *Blood and Belonging*, in which he sets out to explain the rise of contemporary nationalism in places like Croatia, Germany, Ukraine, and Quebec – at a time when he and many other highly educated, thoughtful people had assumed that 'the world was moving irrevocably beyond nationalism, beyond tribalism, beyond the provincial confines of the identities inscribed in our passports, towards a global market culture which was to be our new home'.[208] In this book he asks 'what then is this belonging, and the need for it, which nationalism seems to satisfy so satisfactorily?' Listening to the new nationalists in these diverse places, the profoundly cosmopolitan Ignatieff comes to understand the fear and insecurity behind outbreaks of ethnic violence and demands for national independence. The answer to his question about the appeal of nationalism, he discovers, is that 'Without a nation's protection, everything that an individual values can be rendered worthless. Belonging, on this account, is first and foremost protection from violence'.[209]

Australia today is full of people for whom the nation or the state is not an abstraction at all, but a place of security, within which they are free to be different – but a place to which they know they must explicitly, and in person, swear loyalty. This is the sense of belonging that both Marivic and Marvik express. It is the desire to belong that you can see at citizenship ceremonies, and not just among those from war-ravaged countries like Vietnam or South Sudan. I will swear loyalty to this country, however little of it I know or understand, in exchange for the security and protections that we all need – and which allow some of us to live a cosmopolitan life. Ignatieff came to realise that a cosmopolitan, post-nationalist spirit 'will always depend, in the end, on the capacity of nation states to provide security and civility for their citizens'.[210]

This conception of what Ignatieff calls civic nationalism is no abstraction, and it forces us to pay attention to the way a country may, equally, fail to provide security and civility to some of its people. The Black Lives Matter movements in both the US, but also here in Australia, ask us to acknowledge that there are social groups for whom the state's right to use force is a threat, not a protection. Aboriginal

Australians were not accorded the formal rights of citizens until 1967, and many feel their human rights are still not recognised. We should not expect people to whom we do not offer protection and security to feel that they 'belong' in the same way as every other citizen.

Ignatieff knows that belonging means more than safety. It also means being 'recognized and understood', something that is relatively unproblematic in stable monocultural countries, like the Nordic social democracies until recently, or Japan today:

> To belong is to understand the tacit codes of the people you live with; it is to know that you will be understood without having to explain yourself. People, in short, 'speak your language'.

In a thoroughly unsystematic way I have asked a few people what makes them feel that they belong here. A good friend of mine, a fifth-generation Australian, immediately said that words were so important to her that she could never feel at home in a country that did not speak English, however sympathetic she might be to every other aspect of life there. She then added that she would not feel fully at home anywhere that did not get her jokes (and hers are very good). We agreed that the Australian sense of humour is very distinctive, and sharing it contributes powerfully to our sense of being understood. For people who don't like jokes, clearly this is not going to be important, but it reminded me that some of my most intense moments of feeling happily Australian have occurred when watching Roy and HG commenting on the Olympics, or Sammy J on the State of Hookturnistan during Covid-19 (for Victorians), or Hannah Gadsby talking about her dog, or Bryan Dawe interviewing John Clarke.

Expecting everyone to understand your jokes is a pretty high bar to set for a country with a large-scale immigration program, let alone one bringing particular sensitivities from different cultural communities, but perhaps a sense of humour grows on you over time. I haven't heard any suggestion that a revised citizenship test should include a measure of everyone's sense of humour, but it is perhaps no less silly than asking someone who Donald Bradman was. The revised citizenship test coming into force at the end of 2020 moves the focus from sport to values, and aligns with Ignatieff's concept of civic nationalism, focussing on Australia's democratic institutions and beliefs, as well as individual rights and liberties, including 'equalities'.

Tim Winton would surely support the suggestion made by Thomas Wilson that the citizenship test should include questions about Australia's unique wildlife and natural history. I particularly liked Wilson's recommendation that there be a question about the chuditch (or a quoll, as it would be called on the eastern side of the country), 'a small carnivorous marsupial that is very friendly, although it's (sadly) illegal to keep one as a pet'.[211] The argument that we need to know more about our natural environment has been made with wit and erudition by writers like George Seddon and Don Watson. It is hard to care deeply for and protect something that you don't understand.

***

The material distributed to all new Australian citizens proclaims that 'Citizenship is the bond that unites us all', and at one level this is simply a truism.[212] But there are particular ways in which people are united in different countries, and in some the bonds are more tenuous than others. I have always liked the way civic nationalism – the security and protections offered in exchange for loyalty – has evolved in Australia, and I think that this is where at least one key element of my sense of belonging lies. The reality of citizenship is expressed through the concrete rights that have been won (and lost) at different historical moments through social and political campaigns. They are not guaranteed for ever, and whole libraries of political theory exist about how formal rights can be rendered meaningless by the loss of what the economist and philosopher Amartya Sen calls 'capability'. By this he means what individuals are able to do rather than any passive measures of resource distribution. I feel at home in Australia (the country and the continent) in part because of the distinctive historic rights and protections that exist for citizens: the campaign for the eight-hour day; votes for women; the Harvester judgement, which laid the ground for a fair day's pay for a fair day's work and the concept of a basic wage; the successful integration of huge numbers of post Second World War immigrants without creating a secondary low-pay labour market; the invention of feminist bureaucrats; and compulsory voting and the sausage sizzle.[213] On my reading list for new citizens I would include Judith Brett's recent book about how we vote, *From Secret Ballot to Democracy Sausage*.

Many of the things I admire most have been undermined by the rise of neo-liberal ideas since the 1990s, their enthusiastic promotion by many employers and corporate interests, and their application by governments. I could also list the things which drive some to despair – such as our response to the Uluru Statement from the Heart, and the failure to tackle climate change. But I am not despairing.

The moments of crisis in my sense of where I belong have been relatively few and far between, but I don't wish to sweep the contingent nature of my sense of belonging under the carpet. This sense of contingency is perhaps the fate of accidental immigrants in particular. A long-standing colleague who, like me, arrived from England with a newly minted PhD to start her academic career in Melbourne, went on to occupy a number of significant leadership roles, and in retirement continued to contribute to feminist social policy and the arts through her board memberships. Suddenly confined to Australia by the coronavirus, she finds herself contemplating returning to live in England to be near her elderly siblings and their families, five decades after she left. She told me about this, a feeling that I think took her by surprise, when I added her to my random survey about belonging. At the time I was reading Marivic's comments about how having a baby here tied her to Australia. I do not feel tied to this land in quite the biological way Marivic does, but it is not coincidental that I chose the moment when I had a baby to apply for citizenship; and I remember thinking that I should do this because this baby was going to be Australian.

It turns out that this baby grew up to feel no special attachment to Australia at all, choosing to spend her twenties and early thirties working in London, San Francisco and New York. I was reminded of her attitudes by Thornton McCamish in his book about the enormously successful writer Alan Moorehead. McCamish quotes the letter Neville Shute wrote to Moorehead when they were planning a trip together to Australia in the 1950s:

> So many Australians when they are young seem to find Australia narrow and stultifying, and escape as soon as possible to the larger world. The fact that their birth place happens to be the happiest country in the world to live in doesn't appeal

> to adventurous young people who want to mix in great affairs, and it is only when great affairs begin to pall that one starts looking for the really happy places.[214]

Moorehead was old enough to be open to this point of view. He wrote to his wife that in the 'colonies', Europe seems 'filled with the most splendid and glamorous things, richer than anything in colonial life'.

> Over there is the mirage, the dream-city and the escape. Here one is down to earth and does the washing up. The time is now – there is no past ... Over there the time is past and, seen from this boarding house, it is full of Napoleons and Tintorettos. What the colonial does not realise is that the washing up still has to be done in Europe.

Later in the biography McCamish addresses Moorehead's experience of the outback as he worked on his book *Cooper's Creek*, about the doomed attempt by Burke and Wills to cross Australia from south to north in 1860. It brings back memories of McCamish's own primary school days and the boredom induced by efforts to teach him about the Australian outback. 'We were probably some of the luckiest children on earth, but that didn't occur to me then. All I knew was that Stonehenge and Portuguese forts were elsewhere; in this country it was just dry creeks and bush-band lagerphones.'[215] In the 1980s and 1990s there were still a lot of middle-class primary school children who found the story of the Eureka stockade and opportunities to go gold-panning in Victoria profoundly uninteresting by comparison with stories about Roundheads and Cavaliers.

My daughter returned to Australia with her American husband towards the end of Obama's presidency, the political future uncertain, to have children somewhere less stressful (and less interesting) than Brooklyn. I have Trump to thank for their decision to stay much longer than originally intended. But I think they, and the many other Australians returning to Australia to seek safety in the time of Covid-19, understand that the state is no abstraction. The Australian nation does not have the thrilling revolutionary history of the US or France, but it offers compulsory voting, the administrative management of electoral boundaries, Medicare and compulsory bike helmets.

I had better luck with having an Australian baby the second time around. My son chose Australian History as a final-year subject, after his sister had buried herself in the Chinese and French revolutions and Renaissance art, and he has no doubt at all about his sense of belonging. But there was a time when I wondered what I would do if they both moved to live permanently overseas, and from time to time I discussed this with an American friend whom I met during our children's primary school days. Both her daughters have chosen to leave Australia, probably permanently. The era of cheap and easily available international travel made these dilemmas seem almost theoretical. But now, in our seventies, should we begin to discuss where we would like to be buried – or rather where our ashes should be scattered – rather than where we belong?

I reflect on the tensions about belonging and family (luckily theoretical tensions for me at this particular moment) and the way my mother resolved the same questions. With my father she moved to live in France in her early sixties. Two of her three children had migrated to very distant countries, and the third was tied to a dairy farm at the other end of France, which meant that he too was effectively on another planet. When my father died I told my mother that we would be really happy if she came to live with us here in Melbourne, knowing her affection for the country; and after all, her mother had been Australian – even if she left in 1914.

My mother did not hesitate for a second, despite living alone in her 80s, in a tiny French village in the Béarn. She had come to love the Pyrénées and could not imagine abandoning the view of them from her terrace for any amount of family love and support on the other side of the world. Unlike my mother, I realise that I would hesitate about many things if both my children left this country, and that their absence would seriously threaten my sense of belonging. The landscape would not hold me. Perhaps that is why I decided I needed to find some golden handcuffs for at least one bit of my family.

Reading about an award-winning renovation and extension that was designed for a family in Melbourne as a series of pavilions around a shared central garden – as opposed to the usual addition of a large second storey – I was smitten. I have always liked the idea of living very close to family or close friends, even having them next door with a gate in the back fence between us. But it is hard to pull this off as the right properties rarely come up together, and if they do cost far too much. This project suggested a way to achieve something on one block of land. Perhaps I could create a sort of multi-generational inner urban compound on the same principles as this much-admired, deconstructed family home. We needed to build round the edges of a block, one family at each end, leaving a shared space along one side for larger gatherings and a garden in the middle for competitive tomato production. And this is where I now live.

Notes

1. Frank Moorhouse, *Grand Days*, Random House, Sydney, 1993. Edith Barry lived on in two more novels, *Dark Palace*, 2000 and *Cold Light*, 2011.
2. Brendan Foster, 'When the Rajneeshee sex cult turned Fremantle orange', *WA Today*, 24 March 2017, <www.watoday.com.au>
3. George Seddon, 'A Captive Jungle, or Rainforest in South Yarra', in Andrea Gaynor (ed.), *George Seddon: Selected Writings*, La Trobe University Press, Melbourne, 2019, p. 170, originally published in 1984.
4. Quoted in Seddon, 'A Captive Jungle', p. 170.
5. The Australian Forest Walk was not established until 1991, and only in 2006 was a significant collection of Victorian forest species planted.
6. James Wood, 'On Not Going Home', *London Review of Books*. Vol. 36 No. 4. 20 February 2014.
7. Merriam Webster Dictionary.
8. Published as *Unity and Diversity: The Barton Lectures*, Helen Irving (ed.), ABC Books, Sydney, 2001.
9. *A Divided Working Class*, Constance Lever-Tracy and Michael Quinlan, Routledge and Kegan Paul, London, 1988. If I thought anyone would read it, it would be on my list of books for new citizens.
10. Wood, 'On Not Going Home.'
11. Melbourne led the way in allowing unrestricted weekend trading in the mid-1990s. Perth resisted Sunday trading until 2012.
12. George Seddon, 'Placing the Debate: A Long Postscript', in *Landprints: Reflections on Place and Landscape*, Cambridge University Press, Cambridge, 1997, p. 139.
13. Matthew Colloff, *Landscapes of Our Hearts: Reconciling People and Environment*, Thames and Hudson, Melbourne, 2020, p. 229.
14. Don Watson, *The Bush*, Penguin, Melbourne, 2014, pp. 69–70.
15. Watson, p. 109.
16. Seddon, 'Placing the Debate', p. 118.
17. George Seddon, *The Old Country: Australian Landscapes, Plants and People*, Cambridge University Press, Melbourne, 2006, p. xv.

18 Seddon, 'The Evolution of Perceptual Attitudes', 1976, reproduced in Andrea Gaynor (ed).
19 Quoted in Seddon, 'Perceptual Attitudes', in Gaynor, p. 60.
20 *The Bush*, p. 65
21 Seddon, 'Evolution of Perceptual Attitudes' in Gaynor, p. 63.
22 'Evolution' p. 64.
23 Emma Viskic, 'Rural Australia: The Perfect Setting for Mystery', Crime Reads website, 25 October 2018, <crimereads.com/rural-australia-the-perfect-setting-for-mystery/>.
24 Patrick White, *Tree of Man*, Vintage, Sydney, 2009, p. 169.
25 Jill Ker Conway, *The Road from Coorain*, Minerva, London, 1992, p. 7.
26 Ker Conway, p. 5.
27 Ker Conway p. 25.
28 Eric Rolls, *A Million Wild Acres*, Hale & Iremonger, Sydney, 2011, p. 42.
29 Ker Conway, p. 59.
30 Ker Conway p. 10.
31 Robert Kenny, *Gardens of Fire*, UWA Publishing, Perth, 2013, p. 7.
32 Kenny, p. 8.
33 Ibid.
34 Kenny, p. 17.
35 Kenny, p. 22.
36 Kenny, p. 23.
37 Kenny, p. 24.
38 Ibid.
39 Tom Griffiths, 'We Have Still Not Lived Long Enough', *Inside Story*, 16 February 2009. Extended version with additional ending published by Australian Academy of the Humanities, nd.
40 Seddon, *The Old Country*, p. 189.
41 Michael Pollan, *Second Nature: A Gardener's Education*, Delta, New York, 1991, p. 286.
42 Pollan, *Second Nature*, p. 2.
43 George Seddon, *Sense of Place: A Response to an Environment*, University of Western Australia Press, 1972, p. 262.
44 Seddon, *The Old Country*, p. 83.
45 Ibid.
46 See Seddon on Guilfoyle's vision for the RBG Melbourne, 'A captive jungle, or rainforest in South Yarra', in Gaynor (ed.).
47 Peter Timms (ed.), *The Nature of Gardens*, Allen and Unwin, Sydney, 1999.
48 Belinda Probert, 'How We Shape the Garden', in Peter Timms (ed.), p. 73.
49 Pollan, *Second Nature*, pp. 1–2.
50 A garden dedicated to Australian plants, it was designed by Taylor Cullity Lethlean, with Paul Thompson, and opened in 2006.

51 Georgina Reid, 'Fiona Brockhoff's Sublime Garden Wonderland', The Planthunter website, 26 September 2019, <theplanthunter.com.au/gardens/fiona-brockhoff-karkalla-garden/>.
52 Seddon, *The Old Country*, p. 183.
53 Ken Jennings, 'The Longest Straight Road in the World Is...', Conde Nast Traveler, 26 December 2016, www.cntraveler.com/story/the-longest-straight-road-in-the-world-is.
54 Tim Winton, 'The Island Seen and Felt,' Places Journal, March 2017. Accessed 26 Jan 2021. <https://placesjournal.org/article/the-island-seen-and-felt/>
55 Bruce A Auld, *A Traveller's Flora*, Samara, Borenore, 2013.
56 Kenny, pp. 202–3.
57 Tim Low, *Where Song Began: Australia's Birds and How They Changed the World*, Penguin, Melbourne, 2014, p. 278.
58 Low says that the Australian magpie is 'almost the only large songbird to offer pleasing songs as well as harsh attack calls. Kept around the homesteads to announce intruders, it provided, in effect, the warble of the canary and the bark of the dog' (Tim Low, p. 87).
59 Quoted in Low, p. 7.
60 Op cit, p. 8.
61 Watson, p. 355
62 Low, p. 9.
63 Low, p. 10.
64 Quoted in Low.
65 Low p. 80.
66 Jeffery Boswall, 'The Top 10 British Birdsongs', British Library website, <www.bl.uk/the-language-of-birds/articles/the-top-10-british-birdsongs>.
67 Margaret Kiddle, *Men of Yesterday: A Social History of the Western District of Victoria 1834–1890*, Melbourne University Press, Melbourne, 1961, p. 318.
68 Kiddle, pp. 319–20.
69 Low, *Where Song Began*, p. 255.
70 See for example Jackie French, *Diary of a Wombat*, Clarion Books, New York, 2003. On the other hand, the Pre-Raphaelite painter and poet Dante Gabriel Rossetti was obsessed with wombats, owning two and weeping over their deaths. He was not alone in his enthusiasm for the wombat which was highly prized in nineteenth century Europe. Napoleon owned one as did the Duke of Edinburgh. See John Simons, *Rossetti's Wombat: Pre-Raphaelites and Australian Animals in Victorian London*, Libri Publishing, Farringdon, 2008.
71 Christine Cooper, The Secret Life of Echidnas Reveals a World-class Digger Vital to Our Ecosystems', *The Conversation*, 20 October.
72 '7 things you might not know about Echidnas', from Government of South Australia, Dept of Environment and Water website, Good Living section, 2019, <www.environment.sa.gov.au>.

73 Tom Keneally, 'Australia's groundskeeper' in *Animals Make us Human*, Leah Kaminsky and Meg Keneally (eds), Penguin Life, Melbourne, 2020, p. 62.
74 'Leeches', Australian Museum website, <australian.museum/learn/animals/worms/leeches/>.
75 Watson, *The Bush*, p. 164.
76 Clive Blazey, '"Cultural Cringe" and Our National Garden Identity', the Diggers Club website, <www.diggers.com.au/garden-advice/articles-and-more/articles/trees/rnlc17-natural-garden-identity/>.
77 Megan Gorrey, 'We're Not Nationalistic About It: Sydney Needs Exotic Trees, Light Colour Buildings to Cool Down', *Sydney Morning Herald*, 1 December 2020, <www.smh.com.au>
78 Ian Brooker and David Kleinig, *Eucalyptus: An Illustrated Guide to Identification*, Reed New Holland, Sydney, p. 8.
79 Brooker and Kleinig, *Eucalyptus*, p. 8.
80 'Koalas at Cape Otway', Wildlife Victoria website, <www.wildlife.vic.gov.au/our-wildlife/koalas/koalas-at-cape-otway>
81 Tim Low, p. 16
82 Watson, p. 268.
83 Low, pp. 30–1.
84 Low, p. 15
85 Low, pp. 33–4.
86 Tom Griffiths, 'We Have Still Not Lived Long Enough'.
87 Mark Twain, *Following the Equator*, Chapter 8, https://www.biblioteca.org.ar/libros/167735.pdf, 2008, originally published in 1897.
88 Low, pp. 45–8.
89 Watson, p. 70.
90 Seddon, *Sense of Place*, pp. xiii–xiv.
91 Jason Smith, *Fred Williams in the You Yangs*, exh. cat., Geelong Gallery, 2017, p. 10 and p. 8, <www.geelonggallery.org.au/cms_uploads/docs/fred-williams-in-the-you-yangs_fa_screen.pdf>.
92 Deborah Hart, *Fred Williams: Infinite Horizons*, National Gallery of Australia, Canberra, 2011, pp. 64–66.
93 Miki Perkins and Royce Millar, 'The grass and the stars' *The Age*, 26 July 2020.
94 Royce Millar and Miki Perkins, 'A terrain marked by failure', *The Age*, 25 July 2020, pp. 26–7.
95 Ibid.
96 Bruce Pascoe, *Dark Emu: Aboriginal Australia and the Birth of Agriculture*, Magabala Books, Broome, 2014, p. 2.
97 Lisa Cox, 'Australia the only developed nation on world list of deforestation hotspots', *The Guardian*, 13 January 2021.
98 'Mount Elephant', Visit Victoria website, www.visitvictoria.com/regions/Great-Ocean-Road/Things-to-do/Outdoor-activities/Walking-and-hiking/Mount-Elephant.

99 Watson, p. 89.
100 Margaret Kiddle, *Men of Yesterday*, 1961, chapter 3, 'Occupation'.
101 Quoted in Margaret Kiddle, p. 40
102 Kiddle, p. 44.
103 Richard Zachariah, *The Vanished Land: Disappearing Dynasties of Victoria's Western District*, Wakefield Press, Adelaide, 2017, p. 208.
104 Quoted in Margaret Kiddle, p. 201.
105 Niel Black, quoted in Margaret Kiddle, pp. 468–9.
106 Donald S Garden, 'George Fairbairn', Australian Dictionary of Biography website, <adb.anu.edu.au/biography/fairbairn-george-363>.
107 Harriet Edquist, 'Homesteads of the Western District', in *Designing Place: An Archaeology of the Western District*, Melbourne Books, Melbourne, 2010.
108 Bill Gammage, *The Biggest Estate on Earth: How Aborigines Made Australia*, Allen and Unwin, Sydney, 2012. For an excellent critical review of some of Gammage's broader claims and his uncritical admiration of the ecological principles of Aboriginal land management see Peter Hiscock's 'Creators or Destroyers: the burning questions of human impact in ancient Aboriginal Australia', *Humanities Australia*, vol 5, 2014, pp. 40–51.
109 Reynolds, 'Foreword' to Bill Gammage, p. xxiii.
110 James Boyce, *The Monthly*, December 2011/January 2012.
111 Quoted in Gammage, p. 314.
112 Seddon, p. 147 in Andrea Gaynor.
113 Seddon, p. 62 in Andrea Gaynor.
114 Charles Massy, *The Cry of the Reed Warbler: A New Agriculture – A New Earth*, University of Queensland Press, Brisbane, 2017, p. 2.
115 John McDonald, 'Arthur Streeton Landscapes Star in Impressive Regional Lineup', Sydney Morning Herald website, <www.smh.com.au>.
116 National Gallery of Australia, <nga.gov.au/federation/detail.cfm?WorkID=45168>.
117 Quoted in John McDonald.
118 Tim Bonyhady, 'Streeton's Shriek', *The Monthly*, December 2020/January 2021.
119 Seddon in Andrea Gaynor, p.159.
120 Gammage, p. 34.
121 Kim Mahood, *Position Doubtful: Mapping Landscapes and Memories*, Scribe, Melbourne, p. 26.
122 Seddon, *A Sense of Place*, p. xiv.
123 Richard Haese, 'The Lost Wimmera Years of Sidney Nolan, 1942–44', <www.ngv.vic.gov.au/essay/the-lost-wimmera-years-of-sidney-nolan-1942-44/. Don Watson describes the series as capturing the Wimmera indelibly. (Watson, *The Bush*, p. 164.)

124 Tony Bennett, 'Australians' favourites show Aboriginal art can transcend social divisions and art boundaries', the *Conversation*, 24 August 2020, <theconversation.com/australians-favourites-show-aboriginal-art-can-transcend-social-divisions-and-art-boundaries-143827>. Survey sample included Aboriginal and Torres St Islanders, Italian, Lebanese, Chinese and Indian respondents.
125 Ibid.
126 There is an extremely useful and detailed guide to their identification and recording called *Scarred Trees*, produced by Andrew Long for Aboriginal Affairs Victoria in 2003. <www.aboriginalvictoria.vic.gov.au/sites/default/files/2019-09/Scarred-Trees_0.pdf>
127 Jan Critchett, *A Distant Field of Murder: Western District Frontiers 1834–1848*, Melbourne University Press, Melbourne, 1992.
128 Richard Broome, *Aboriginal Victorians, A History Since 1800*, Allen and Unwin, Sydney, 2005, p. 81.
129 'Casterton', *Sydney Morning Herald* website, 8 February 2004, <www.smh.com.au>.
130 Ross Gibson in *Designing Place*.
131 William Westgarth, *Australia Felix; or, a Historical and Descriptive Account of the Settlement of Port Phillip, New South Wales*, 1848, quoted in Harriet Edquist, 'Stony Rises: The Formation of a Cultural Landscape', in *Designing Place*.
132 'Constance "Connie" Hart', Aboriginal Victoria website, www.aboriginalvictoria.vic.gov.au/constance-connie-hart.
133 'This project will develop geospatial methods to uncover and document the technological foundations of the aquaculture complex, and contribute to the understanding of the Gunditjmara technological knowledge and history.' Australian Research Council grant SR200200227.
134 Shona Martyn, 'I'm Hoping It's a Blip: Sales Down in Difficult Year for Publishing Industry', *Sydney Morning Herald website*, 10 January 2020, <www.smh.com.au>.
135 Billy Griffiths, *Deep Time Dreaming: Uncovering Ancient Australia*, Black Inc, Melbourne 2018.
136 Billy Griffiths, pp. 279–80.
137 David Christian, *Maps of Time: An Introduction to Big History*, University of California Press, Berkeley, 2004; on Audible 'Big History: The Big Bang, Life on Earth, and the Rise of Humanity', produced for *The Great Courses*.
138 Griffiths, p. 293.
139 Zachariah, *The Vanished Land*, p. 1.
140 Harriet Edquist 'Homesteads of the Western District', in *Designing Place*, p. 128. For a more rose-tinted view see *Great Properties of Country Victoria, The Western District's Golden Age*, by Richard Allen and Kimbal Baker, The Miegunyah Press, Melbourne, 2015.
141 Kiddle, pp. 311–315.

142 Chloe Hooper, *The Engagement*, Penguin, Melbourne, 2014, p. 10 and then p. 45.
143 Zachariah, p. 183.
144 Rosalind Smallwood, *Hard to Go Bung: World War 2 Settlement in Victoria 1945–1962*, Australian Scholarly Publishing, Melbourne, 2011, p. 17.
145 Smallwood, p. 138.
146 Translated by Russell Ward, *Socialism without Doctrine*, Alternative Publishing Co-operative, Sydney, 1977.
147 Zachariah, p. 65.
148 In 2014 the Warnambool Cheese and Butter company was bought, after a fierce bidding war, by a Canadian dairy company worth $10.6 billion. Jane Harper, 'How Saputo Won the War for Control of Warrnambool Cheese and Butter', *Herald Sun* website, 25 January 2014, www.heraldsun.com.au/business/how-saputo-won-the-war-for-control-of-warrnambool-cheese-and-butter/news-story/9f480362996788b2418c3caa52a11d0e.
149 Danielle Grindlay, 'Port of Portland now biggest exporter of blue gum hard woodchips in the world', 18 August 2015. <www.abc.net.au/news/rural/2015-08-18/blue-gum-portland-woodchips-exports-china-japan-forestry/6704158>
150 Larry Schlesinger, 'Historic Mawallok Estate up for Sale', 7 October 2019, <www.afr.com/property/commercial/historic-mawallok-estate-up-for-sale-20191007-p52ybl>.
151 Sue Neales, 'Fibre King', *Agjournal*, August 2020, p. 33.
152 'Don't Let Them Pull the Wool!', Edgar's Mission website, <www.edgarsmission.org.au> Planning Application: 19/0110 Use and development of intensive animal production (sheep production and dairy) at 1440 Inverleigh-Winchelsea Road, Inverleigh. info@surfcoast.vic.gov.au.
153 Dairy Australia, 'Dairy Farming in South West Australia: An Investment Guide', 2017.
154 Lesley Hughes, The Milk of Human Genius', *The Monthly*, March 2020.
155 Lesley Hughes.
156 See Michael Pollan, *The Omnivore's Dilemma: A Natural History of Four Meals*, Penguin, New York, 2006.
157 Massy, *The Call of the Reed Warbler*.
158 Tony Ellwood, Foreword to *Heartlands and Headwaters*, National Gallery of Victoria, Melbourne, 2015.
159 Ross Garnaut, *Superpower*, La Trobe University Press, Melbourne, 2019, p. 143.
160 Tom Griffiths, *The Art of Time Travel: Historians and Their Craft*, Black Inc, Melbourne, 2016, p. 159.
161 Winton, 'The island seen and felt', p. 5.

162 Winton, p. 5.
163 Winton, p. 10.
164 Mahood, *Position Doubtful*, p. 9.
165 Mahood, *Position Doubtful*, p. 2.
166 Mahood, *Craft for a Dry Lake*, Penguin Random House, Sydney, 2012, p. 33.
167 Ker Conway, p. 5.
168 Mahood, *Craft for a Dry Lake*, pp. 86–9.
169 Mahood, *Craft for a Dry Lake*, p. 252.
170 Mahood, *Craft for a Dry Lake*, p. 258.
171 After a series of wet years in the 1980s and 1990s, drought took hold across south-east Australia. Temperatures rose. As scientific warnings mounted of an impending climate catastrophe, Boyer's work focused on the local ecological effects of global warming in the Binalong district. One of Boyer's major works was the *Time Change* animation completed in 2006. Using a series of watercolour works, the powerful and at times whimsical animation shows the life of a female farmer in the Binalong district in the future, when global warming has profoundly altered patterns of farm activity and the land.
172 'Diana Boyer Environmental art collection', National Museum Australia website, <www.nma.gov.au>.
173 Tim Winton, p. 8.
174 George Seddon, The *Old Country*, p. 193.
175 Tim Winton, p. 5
176 Peter Read, *Belonging: Australians, Place and Aboriginal Ownership*, Cambridge University Press, Melbourne, 2000, pp. 186–7.
177 Peter Read, p. 178.
178 Winton, p. 6
179 Kim Mahood, *Position Doubtful* p. 5
180 Kim Mahood, p. 296.
181 Saskia Beudel, *A Country in Mind: Memoir with Landscape*, UWA Publishing, Perth, 2013, p. 91.
182 Beudel, p. 52
183 Quoted in Read, p. 14.
184 Peter Read, p. 5.
185 Quoted in Read, pp. 191–9.
186 Quoted in Read, p. 189.
187 Mahood, *Position Doubtful*, p. 288.
188 Quoted in Read, p. 138.
189 Quoted in Read, p. 141.
190 Quoted in Read, p. 157
191 Ghassan Hage, 'On other belongings' in *Joyful Strains: Making Australia Home*, eds Kent MacCarter and Ali Lemer, Affirm Press, Melbourne, 2013.
192 This idea is explored in much greater depth in an article called 'Another de-colonial politics is possible', published on his Blog, *Hage*

     Ba'a, December 2018, http://hageba2a.blogspot.com/2018/12/another-de-colonial-politics-is-possible.html
193 Nicholas Rothwell, *Wings of the Kite-Hawk*, Picador, Sydney, 2003, p. 193.
194 Mark McKenna, *Looking for Blackfella's Point: An Australian History of Place*, UNSW Press, Sydney, 2014, p. 14.
195 George Seddon, *The Old Country*, p. 166
196 Patrice Newell, *Ten Thousand Acres: A Love Story*, Lantern, Penguin Books, Melbourne, 2006. In this book she describes twenty years of biodynamic farming on the property she shares with Phillip Adams, and her work identifying and restoring native plants and vegetation.
197 Bill Gammage, *The Great Estate*, p. 323.
198 Winton, p. 10.
199 'Fauna Extinction Listings May Jump 14 Per Cent After 2019–20 Fires. Full version at Ward, M., Tulloch, A.I.T., Radford, J.Q. *et al.* 'Impact of 2019–2020 mega-fires on Australian fauna habitat', *Nat Ecol Evol* 4, 1321–1326 (2020).
200 George Seddon, *The Old Country*, p. 240.
201 Mark McKenna, *Looking for Blackfella's Point*, p. 223, p. 8.
202 Peter Read, p. 140
203 Peter Read, p. 223, p. 204.
204 Peter Read, p. 210. p. 223.
205 Quoted in Billy Griffiths, p. 203.
206 Ibid.
207 Kim Mahood, *Position Doubtful*, p. 2.
208 Michael Ignatieff, *Blood and Belonging: Journeys Into the New Nationalism*, Vintage, London, 1994, p. 2.
209 Michael Ignatieff, *Blood and Belonging*, p. 6.
210 Ignatieff, *Blood and Belonging*, p. 9.
211 'Australia's natural history and native species should be on the citizenship test', Thomas Wilson, the *Conversation* 25 September 2020, <theconversation.com>.
212 *Australian Citizenship: Our Common Bond*, Commonwealth of Australia 2018.
213 Judith Brett, *From Secret Ballot to Democracy Sausage: How Australia Got Compulsory Voting*, Text, Melbourne, 2019.
214 Thornton McCamish, *Our Man Elsewhere: In Search of Alan Moorehead*, Black Inc., Melbourne, 2016, p. 182.
215 Thornton McCamish, pp. 244–5.

The publisher and author thank the following for permission to quote from their works. All bibliographical information is listed in full in the Notes.

Allen and Unwin:
Bill Gammage

Black Inc. Books:
Billy Griffiths
Thornton McCamish

Magabala Books:
Bruce Pascoe

Penguin Random House Australia:
Chloe Hooper
Tim Low
Don Watson

Scribe Publications:
Kim Mahood

UWA Publishing:
Saskia Beudel
Robert Kenny

Acknowledgements

I should begin by acknowledging that it was my son, Owen, who forced my hand after all my talk of buying a place in the country; who wouldn't let me chicken out or buy somewhere on the outskirts of a country town. As we drove away from inspecting the one that finally seemed right, he promised he would learn to drive if I bought it. Fortunately I didn't count on this.

I might also never have done this had I not made myself deeply unpopular with my employer when I was old enough to throw in the towel but young enough to take on a rural project.

I would have learned a lot less from this plan to learn to feel at home in the country had I not found myself in a small community of generous and wise neighbours who helped when my pump broke down, lent me their brush cutters and chain saws until I had my own, let me seed my dam with their yabbies, and showed me where the jack jumpers were living. For sheer muscle power I relied greatly on Ross Brooker and on Chris Harris for landscaping.

I would know little about the Western District and its pastoral history were it not for the friendship and hospitality of Edwina Cornish and her mother Cecily. And I have repaid this with relentless critical questioning.

As can be seen from this book my learning to live in the Antipodes has been immeasurably enriched over four decades by the works of some key writers. Writers like George Seddon and Michael Pollan showed me ways to think about landscapes and gardening that were multi-dimensional, enlightening and also funny. I have been in conversation with them – in my head – for a couple of decades, albeit in a desultory fashion. I liked the idea of one day sitting down and working out and then writing about my own experiences of trying to become an Australian at home on this continent.

For the fact that I did eventually sit down and wrestle my thoughts onto paper I can thank SARS-CoV-2, or the coronavirus. When Victorian Premier Daniel Andrews announced the second full lockdown for Victoria in July 2020 I decided to sit in my newly built library and write 1000 words every day. I figured I would run out of things to say by the time we were allowed out again. I knew that if I didn't get going immediately I probably never would.

What I did not expect was the excitement of writing (a feeling that I do not readily associate with the academic writing I have done). Gradually my writing table filled up with books and articles from off my shelves that I wanted to discuss or use to develop my own often incoherent feelings. This kind of writing was a new experience that combined intellectual engagement with everything from archaeology to agriculture with getting to know myself better. I could not wait to get into the library each morning. I didn't quite stay in my pyjamas all day, but pretty close. Lock-down replaced the need to exercise self-discipline on several fronts.

I don't believe anyone writes that many words without hoping that someone will publish them, but it felt a bit like a vanity project. I sent the first five or six thousand of them to Terri-ann White, and she responded immediately by telling me to 'keep writing'. Nothing more, nothing less. As more pages appeared, she maintained this consistent position of unwavering enthusiasm, until I thought I had finished. At that point she started to make me dig a little deeper. She made me think about why I had done certain things or felt certain emotions, and pushed me out of my English reticence. She questioned my regard for one or two of my favourite authors, and alerted me to the fact that I only seemed to admire male landscape writers. She provoked me to look beyond my own bookshelves and belatedly discover Kim Mahood's remarkable memoirs. I now understand why so many writers have wanted to be published by Terri-ann.

It seemed wise to ask someone who was also an immigrant but who did not necessarily share my country enthusiasms to read the manuscript to see if it resonated more widely. Jean Holland, who grew up in Michigan, arrived in Australia around the same time I did, and we met when our children attended the same primary school. She read the first draft with the most generous attention and interest and was an invaluable sounding board.

Over Zoom I told Jane-Frances Kelly what I was doing – a Scot who, as she describes it, fell in love with Australia when she came to work here in her thirties. She suggested I read two books which she had, and we arranged a masked and socially distanced handover when allowed out on our rationed exercise hour. Without her I would not have read Ghassan Hage's illuminating small piece 'On other belongings'.

My mother wrote an eloquent account of her mother's life in the form of a letter to one of her American grand-daughters who had been given the middle name Lilla, in respectful memory of her Australian great-grandmother. These American Proberts knew their English and Caribbean origins, but my mother realised that without this account her grand-daughter might never really know much about the admirable woman behind the name Lilla, let alone the country she came from.

I have a young grand-daughter who is both American and Australian and who also has this middle name. For now she lives in Melbourne, but providing Trump stays out of the White House, she may do a lot of growing up in America. I hope that one day this book may help her understand the Australian side of her family and the remarkable continent where she was born. The best photographs in this book were taken by her father, Ed Blake. The photo of the new fish trap at Budj Bim was taken by one of her grandfathers, Richard Gillespie. The rest of the images are simply personal snaps that capture my life in the country and my travels around Victoria and across the Nullarbor. Thank you to Terri-ann for using them and placing them.

Taking the long view, this book is for Naomi Lilla May and Emilia Charlotte, their mother Henrietta and their uncle Owen.

About Upswell

Upswell Publishing was established in 2021 by Terri-ann White as a not-for-profit press. A perceived gap in the market for distinctive literary works in fiction, poetry and narrative non-fiction was the motivation. In her years as a bookseller, writer and then publisher, Terri-ann has maintained a watch on literary books and the way they insinuate themselves into a cultural space and are then located within our literary and cultural inheritance. She is interested in making books to last: books with the potential to still be noticed, and noted, after decades and thus be ripe to influence new literary histories.

About this typeface

Book designer Becky Chilcott chose Foundry Origin not only as a strong, carefully considered, and dependable typeface, but also to honour her late friend and mentor, type designer Freda Sack, who oversaw the project. Designed by Freda's long-standing colleague, Stuart De Rizzario, much like Upswell Publishing, Foundry Origin was created out of the desire to say something new.